99 Ways to Lead and Succeed

Strategies and Stories for School Leaders

Howard J. Bultinck and Lynn H. Bush

Taylor & Francis Group
New York London

First published 2009 by Eye On Education

Published 2013 by Routledge
711 Third Avenue, New York, NY, 10017, USA
2 Park Square, Milton Park, Abingdon, Oxon OX14 4RN

Routledge is an imprint of the Taylor & Francis Group, an informa business

Copyright © 2009 Taylor & Francis.

All rights reserved. No part of this book may be reprinted or reproduced or utilised in any form or by any electronic, mechanical, or other means, now known or hereafter invented, including photocopying and recording, or in any information storage or retrieval system, without permission in writing from the publishers.

Notices
No responsibility is assumed by the publisher for any injury and/or damage to persons or property as a matter of products liability, negligence or otherwise, or from any use of operation of any methods, products, instructions or ideas contained in the material herein.

Practitioners and researchers must always rely on their own experience and knowledge in evaluating and using any information, methods, compounds, or experiments described herein. In using such information or methods they should be mindful of their own safety and the safety of others, including parties for whom they have a professional responsibility.

Product or corporate names may be trademarks or registered trademarks, and are used only for identification and explanation without intent to infringe.

Library of Congress Cataloging-in-Publication Data

Bultinck, Howard J.
  99 ways to lead and succeed: strategies and stories for school leaders / Howard J. Bultinck and Lynn H. Bush.
    p. cm.
  ISBN 978-1-59667-118-8
  1. Educational leadership. 2. School management and organization. I. Bush, Lynn H. II. Title. III. Title: Ninety-nine ways to lead and succeed.
  LB2805.B875 2009
  371.2—dc22
                                                            2009016749

ISBN 978-1-59667-118-8 (pbk)

Also Available from EYE ON EDUCATION

**Get Organized!
Time Management for School Leaders**
Frank Buck

**What Great Principals Do *Differently*:
15 Things That Matter Most**
Todd Whitaker

**Leadership Connectors:
Six Keys to Developing Relationships in Schools**
Phyllis Ann Hensley and LaVern Burmeister

Creating the High Schools of Our Choice
Tim Westerberg

Professional Development: What Works
Sally J. Zepeda

**Motivating and Inspiring Teachers: The Educational
Leader's Guide for Building Staff Morale, Second Edition**
Todd Whitaker

**Creating School Cultures That Embrace Learning:
What Successful Leaders Do**
Tony Thacker, John S. Bell, and Franklin Schargel

The Principalship from A to Z
Ron Williamson and Barbara R. Blackburn

**The High-Trust Classroom:
Raising Achievement from the Inside Out**
Lonnie Moore

Applying Servant Leadership in Today's Schools
Mary K. Culver

**People First: The School Leader's Guide to Building
and Cultivating Relationships with Teachers**
Jennifer Hindman, Angela Seiders, and Leslie Grant

About the Cover

School leaders and their constituents could certainly learn from migrating geese. Lessons might include working toward a common vision, staying the course and trusting one another, sharing leadership tasks and recognizing that we all have unique talents, encouraging and supporting each other, and sticking together during challenging school times.

We thank Dr. Robert McNiesch, science teacher and school administrator, who first wrote about migrating geese in 1972. For the full story we refer you to http://suewidemark.com/lessonsgeese.htm#anon.

Dedication

For my wife, Nancy, and my three children, Christopher, Nicholas, and Stephanie, who always made me look better than I ever was or hope to be.

Howard

For Guy and (the late Arline) Franzese who were my first teachers and leaders.

For my husband, Jack, and my children, Peter and Abby.

Lynn

Meet the Authors

Howard J. Bultinck, a former principal and superintendent, is an assistant professor in the Department of Educational Leadership and Development at Northeastern Illinois University (NEIU), Chicago, Illinois. Prior to coming to Northeastern, he worked at Sunset Ridge School District #29 in Northfield, Illinois, where he served as superintendent/principal for 24 years. Additionally, he has served as a business manager, elementary school teacher, and as Midwestern Advertising Manager for *Instructor Magazine*. Howard Bultinck has a Ph.D. from Northwestern University, Evanston, Illinois, in Administration and Policy studies, a post M.S. program of study in Curriculum and Instruction from Northwestern University, an M.S. degree in educational administration from National College of Education, Evanston, Illinois, and a B.S. Ed. degree in Elementary Education from Northern Illinois University, De Kalb, Illinois. Howard has published articles and presented nationally on school leadership topics.

Lynn H. Bush, a former principal and central office administrator, is an associate professor in the Department of Educational Leadership and Development at Northeastern Illinois University (NEIU), Chicago, Illinois. Prior to coming to NEIU, Lynn served as a central office administrator in curriculum and instruction, preschool/elementary, elementary, middle school principal. Her professional career began as a middle school language arts teacher. Lynn has a Ph.D. from the University of Illinois (Chicago), Chicago, Illinois, in Curriculum and Instruction, an M.A in Curriculum and Instruction and Educational Leadership from Loyola University, Chicago, Illinois, and a B.S.Ed. in Elementary Education from Drake University Des Moines, Iowa. Lynn has published articles and presented nationally on school leadership topics.

Acknowledgements

Writing a book is a team effort, especially for first-time authors, and we have many people to thank. To begin, we want to express gratitude to the people whose stories are mentioned in our book: Ken Addison; Mike Arnold; Bill Attea; Hank Bangser; Ted Bargmann; John Beckwith; Mary Bortz; George Bravos; Betty Brockelman; Jennifer Budd; Mary Brown; Frank and Lynn Fiarito; Gary Fry; Joan Goodwin; Fred Gougler; Homer Harvey; William Hazard; Paul Jung; Pam Kennedy; Peg Lee; Ron Levitsdy; Dan Lortie; Guadalupe Martinez; Rich Miller; Renee Montero; Min Namkung; Mary Osborne; Dave Parks; Ken Priban; Bob Polster; Becca Sita; Dr. and Mrs. Sita; George Steffen; Rick Walters; and Charles Young. These administrators, managers, teachers, students, parents, university colleagues, professionals, and friends have deepened our knowledge of school leadership and its application. Their interactions with us have allowed us to reflect on our practice and draw conclusions on what being a school leader means.

The school districts where we worked as educators provided us with opportunities to patiently hone our craft over our lifetime, for which we are most grateful. Specifically, we would like to mention Lincolnwood School District #74, Lincolnwood, Illinois; Sunset Ridge School District #29, Northfield, Illinois; Oak Lawn-Hometown School District #123, Oak Lawn, Illinois; New Buffalo Unit School District, New Buffalo, Michigan; Aurora School District #131, Aurora, Illinois; Orland Park School District #135, Orland Park, Illinois; Elmwood Park School District #401, Elmwood Park, Illinois; and St. Charles CUSD #303, St. Charles, Illinois.

We also would like to thank the faculty in the Department of Educational Leadership, Northeastern Illinois University, Chicago, Illinois, for support we received from colleagues, including Bonnie Chauncey, Florina Sirb, John Sullivan, and Zipporah Robinson. Without their kindness, support, humor, and expertise our book would have not come to fruition. Many thanks also to our professional organization, National Association of Elementary School Principals (NAESP), for its speedy email responses, which provided answers to very specific questions.

Additionally, thanks to our publisher, Bob Sickles, who has made the process of writing this book a pleasure right from the beginning with his support, guidance, and direction. Whenever we had a question, Bob was there with a timely response. His counsel and personal interest in our work and care for education made a significant difference in our lives.

Finally thanks to our family who understood that we would be spending long hours at the computer writing and editing drafts, sending and receiving emails, and pondering over each and every word in the manuscript.

Contents

Meet the Authors vi
Acknowledgements vii
Foreword xii
Introduction xiii

1   On Being a Dynamic Leader 1
    Ask for Frequent Feedback. 6
    Be Wary of Your Achilles Heel. 7
    Befriend the Best. 8
    Come to Understand Slowly—But Only if Time Permits. 9
    Dare to Be Different. 11
    Don't Be a One-Hit Wonder. 12
    Engage the Broader School Community. 13
    Fine-Tune Your Acting Abilities. 14
    Foster Purposeful and Consistent Communication. 15
    Know Everyone's Name and Then Some. 17
    Mind Your Mouth. 18
    Prioritize Using the Three "P" Philosophy. 19
    Reach Out to Uninvolved Parents. 20
    Seize the Lead in Challenging Times. 21
    Take a Lickin' and Keep on Tickin'. 22
    Take Rumor and Hearsay in Stride. 24
    Think Beyond Today. 26
    Treasure School Rituals, Ceremonies, and Traditions. 27
    Tune into the Politics. 28
    Value Parents as Allies. 29

2   On Becoming a Moral and Ethical Leader 31
    Answer to Yourself First. 35
    Care Deeply. 36
    Create a Climate of Confidence. 38
    Don't Undo Your Life's Work. 39
    Establish an Ethic of Compassion. 40
    Exercise the Powers of a Superhero. 41
    Experience Empathy. 42
    Gain Acceptance by Making Moral and Ethical Decisions. 43
    Have a Steadfast System of Beliefs. 44
    Lead with Your Moral Compass. 45

Listen to Your Mother. 45
Protect Your Bonds of Trust. 46
Respect Everyone. 47
Seek and Discover the Truth from Complaints. 48
Stand Up for Integrity. 50
Stay the Moral Ground. 51
Take the Honesty Test. 52
Tell the Truth, the Whole Truth, and Nothing but the Truth. 54
Value and Demonstrate Appreciation for Others. 55

3 On Dealing with Stress 57
Act Calm, Cool, and Collected. 62
Agree Politely to Disagree and Be a Broken Record. 63
Attempt to Eat Healthy. 64
Avoid Paranoia. 66
Balance Work and Home, But at Best It's 80/20. 67
Buy Term Life Insurance and Hope Your Term Does Not Come Up. 69
Discover Your Sense of Humor. 70
Do Crossword Puzzles, Sudoku, Word Jumbles, and More. 71
Don't Burn the Candle at Both Ends 73
Exercise Regularly. 74
Facilitate a Common Sense Solution. 75
Find a Compadre. 77
Get Everyone Involved Rather Than Upset. 78
Learn to Live with a Full Plate. 79
Leave Your Ego at the Front Door. 81
Let "It" Go. 82
Live with a Little Loneliness. 84
Schedule an Annual Physical Exam Whether or
    Not You Think You Need One. 85
Suck It Up on the Tough Days. 86
Try Not to Be Too Hard on Yourself. 87
Use Sunday Evenings to Prepare for the Week. 88
When You Wake Up Tired, Remember at Least You Woke Up. 90

4 On Staying Alive 93
Acknowledge When You Have Made a Mistake. 98
Act as If Each Day Were Your Last. 99
Be Lavish in Your Praise and Miserly in Your Criticism. 100
Become Teflon. 101
Being Right Is Overrated. 103
Break Bread. 104
Can't Please People All of the Time, But You Certainly Can Try. 106

    Come Early, Stay Late, and Don't Do Your Income Tax at Work............ 107
    Deal with the Data Flood.. 108
    Don't Be a Product of Buzzword Bingo. 109
    Expect the Ripple Effect...111
    Find Challenges Before Someone Finds Them for You................................113
    Grow to Be a Change Agent or Change Your Address. 114
    Leverage Technology to Your Advantage. 116
    Navigate the Waters with Barracudas in Mind. 118
    Purchase Your Back-to-School Survival Supplies. 119
    Remember That You Have Three Envelopes, But Only
        Open Two of Them. 121
    Reserve Your Judgments. 122
    Resist the Resistors. 123
    Stretch Yourself by Thinking in Alternatives... 125

5 On Honoring Yourself 127
    Arrange Your Environment So It Reflects You. 131
    Be Upfront, Close, and Personal When Choosing Your Heroes. 133
    Celebrate Your Versatility. 135
    Connect the Dots. 136
    Create Your Own Wristband. 138
    Embody Your School. 139
    Establish an Anecdotal File on Yourself. 140
    Ground Yourself in Reflective Thinking. 142
    Juggle with Scarves Before You Try Torches... 143
    Keep Your Perspective. 144
    Laugh at Yourself... 146
    Learn to Take a Compliment.. 148
    Leave a Forwarding Address.. 149
    Leave Your (Trade) Mark. 150
    Look Like a Professional... 152
    Make a Difference in the Lives of Your Students. 153
    Plan a Vacation a Year in Advance. 154
    Safeguard the Public Trust by Remembering You
        Are *In Loco Parentis*. 157

References 159

Foreword

I have long believed that our schools could be transformed overnight if only the educators within them could and would disclose their abundant craft knowledge so that other practitioners could benefit from their insights.

This is precisely what Howard Bultinck and Lynn Bush have done here. This book is plucked from the fertile fields of their experience as school leaders, the "artichoke hearts" of their professional lives. I find *99 Ways to Lead and Succeed* to be a most impressive display of teamwork, of courage, and insight, all crafted from their rich years of providing leadership for public schools. It is a heroic accomplishment.

Roland Barth

Introduction

99 Ways to Lead and Succeed: Strategies and Stories for School Leaders offers a multitude of concrete and specific suggestions, each accompanied with a personal story, to assist school leaders in becoming more successful in their daily work in schools and in their own personal lives. These tips and strategies are meant for all school leaders, be they school administrators or teacher leaders. The book is reader-friendly in that every suggestion is approximately one to two pages in length, thus not requiring hours of concentrated reading. You can read this book in short stints, or consume it all at once if you so desire.

The five chapters focus on dynamic leadership, moral and ethical leadership, dealing with stress, keeping your job, and being true to and honoring yourself. The tips were not written in any special order. We chose to list them alphabetically by chapter for simplicity and future access. The book concludes with a "Reflection Section," which is simply an area for you to jot down ideas or notes while "reflecting" on how you can best implement the ideas or what they specifically mean to you.

We realize that as school leaders you formulate your own personal framework of leadership in which to operate struggle and be challenged and, hopefully, be successful every day. We also understand that one's leadership style evolves over time and our desire is that this book will provide you with several ideas to reflect upon your own personal framework of practice and enhance it. We trust that will you find these suggestions of value and consider implementing them in your daily routines. It is our desire that you will be a more successful and happier school leader for having read this book. After all, we can always get a little bit better professionally and personally every day.

This book began as a project three years ago when we noticed that our graduate students in school leadership enjoyed hearing our personal suggestions for success and the stories that would accompany them. Our combined multiple experiences in teaching and school leadership spanned large and small school districts in urban, rural, and suburban settings. Our credibility with our students was enhanced because our combined experiences includes teaching in multiple grade levels, as well as being head teacher and team leader. Our experiences also include a wide range of administrative positions—administrative assistant, principalships, curriculum directors, business manager, and superintendent of schools. We are real people with real stories based upon seven decades of experience helping educators bridge the gap between theory and practice.

Our routine in writing the book was to identify the tip and its primary writer and then review the draft work together. Because the suggestions and stories were written independently, you will notice different gender references. The tips and stories are snapshots in time during our lives and come from a variety of settings, numerous colleagues and individuals, and a wide range of experiences and perspectives. We are also both parents with deep commitments to our families, which surfaces from time to time in our stories. We honestly and sincerely enjoyed writing this book. It comes from the heart and is written from experience in a profession to which we are committed to and that we are honored to be part of.

We hope you enjoy our book and that your life as a school leader and as a person will be more enhanced and rewarded by your reading of it.

Howard and Lynn

1
On Being a Dynamic Leader

Schools need classroom teachers and administrators who are dynamic leaders. Research abounds with the qualities, characteristics, behaviors and traits that are needed to become a successful school leader (Sergiovanni, 2005; Goleman, 1995; Lambert, 1998; Barth, 1990). Kimbrough and Nunnery (1988) generalize by saying that leaders tend to possess slightly above average intelligence, as well as important personal and administrative skills, but possession of those skills does not guarantee success as a school leader, nor does lack of these skills rule out success. What the research has found, however, is that it is almost impossible to assign any list of traits to all persons in positions of leadership, including school leadership.

The definition of school leadership is neither a clearly defined path nor a well-constructed concept. There are many viewpoints about how leaders should lead, what skills and traits leaders should have, who should lead and who should be led, when to lead and when to be led. New school leaders need to formulate their own personal framework of leadership in which to operate. Hopefully the path is lively, energetic, and vibrant, culminating in a successful school leadership experience.

So what makes a school leader dynamic? Although a charismatic leader can have short-term success, a dynamic leader sustains school improvement over a long period of time (Deming, 1997; Hargreaves & Fullan,1998). A dynamic leader can be defined as one who leads with "professional vitality"—a profound term that helps to explain the meaning of *dynamic leadership*. Harvey and Donaldson (2003) explain *professional vitality* as:

Passion—a strong inner sense of purpose;

Vigor—mental, physical, and emotional energy;

Facility—"savvy" and skill at the job; and

Satisfaction—a sense of pleasure, accomplishment, and fulfillment.

Passion in dynamic leadership can be reflected in educators as presented in the stories of Mary Osborne and Pam Kennedy, both first grade teachers who embody all that is good and right in our profession. Mary retired over two decades ago after forty-two years in teaching and to this day frequently thinks about those wonderful years of teaching with *her* children. For many of those years, Mary also simultaneously served as principal of her K-3 building. Pam, a recent retiree, is also a daily reminder to all who come within her sphere that the focus of teaching and learning must always be on the children. Her sense of commitment and caring never faltered even when confronted with life's most difficult and personal challenges. When one entered her classroom it was readily apparent children were excited about learning, on task, and felt happy to be there. Children were always at the center of her universe.

Vigor in dynamic leadership is exemplified by the temperament of recently retired Betty Brockelman. Betty is a high-energy central office administrator who works with numerous teachers, students, and parents during the course of her day. Directing curriculum and instruction for a large high school district requires immense energy, poise, and stamina. Betty never strays from her sense of purpose as she keeps educators focused. With tasks, conversations and pressures to design the best curriculum resources for teachers to use, Betty flies high. Her energy is boundless and she generates enthusiasm for the difficult tasks of providing the right curriculum materials for the right students.

Facility in dynamic leadership can be seen daily in the person of Hank Bangser, a recently retired superintendent of one of the highest performing high schools in the nation. His poise, presence, and particular attention to detail are readily observed in daily encounters. He understands the nature and essence of diplomacy while never wavering from the District's mission and purpose as it relates to children. He views the teacher as leader and empowers that person in the daily decision-making processes of the classroom and school.

Satisfaction in dynamic leadership is represented in the school life of Hector Quintana, a recently appointed principal and former assistant principal of an elementary school in the Chicago Public School system in which he taught. Hector almost left his school to find a leadership position. When a position became available at his school, he jumped at it. Hector excels in this position because of his dedication to the students and the community. He derives satisfaction and radiates energy, care, and compassion for children, which provides him with a sense of purpose and fulfillment. Hector exemplifies those educators who love what they do and wouldn't want to be doing anything else.

Additionally a dynamic leader needs the will and commitment to improve education in spite of everyday obstacles. When a leader is not dynamic the organization remains stagnant and the organizational energy, grounded in unproductive human behavior, is essentially wasted. As we search for more useful definitions of leadership and dynamic leadership specifically, one definition of leadership discusses leaders as individuals who significantly affect the thoughts, feelings, and behaviors of a considerable number of people (Gardner, 1995). Of interest in this definition is the concern that leaders can be both a negative and a positive influence. It is that projection of light or darkness in which people live and work, and given the opportunity, improve and move forward. For example, Gardner cited Hitler as a charismatic leader who misused power and position whereas Martin Luther King was a charismatic leader who positively lead and affected social change.

Dynamic school leadership is both a responsibility and a privilege. It is a responsibility because by position leaders have the fate of others in their hands. This trust placed in the leader is earned over time through meaningful relationships and positive interactions. It is a privilege because of the nature and opportunity to provide service to others and serve along with others. For example, dynamic leaders nurture and value the personal needs of others, whereas nondynamic leaders are lethargic in their relationships, listless in their commitment, and characterized by minimalist mentality.

Dynamic school leadership requires school followership. Without followership individuals will wander around aimlessly, wasting valuable school time, resulting in children losing valuable learning opportunities. Simply stated, leaders do not exist without followers. As M.J. Edelman (1977) states: "Leaders lead, followers follow, and the organization prospers." But this simple statement can be misinterpreted. Educators who consider themselves school leaders must do more than simply hold the position of teacher, team leader, department chair or school administrator. Although the power of the position cannot be ignored, by itself position power is not enough. Successful leadership requires having followers who believe in their leader and the organization's mission while engaging in this leadership–followership relationship with trust and confidence.

Dynamic school leadership speaks to a broader audience than just individuals who lead. It is the sum total of experiences, values, and connections among individuals in the school community. This surge of energy and enthusiasm pulls educators into the work of leadership, which naturally leads to improving a school.

What do you think are the fundamentals necessary for dynamic leadership? Do you know dynamic leadership when you see it? Do you owe a professional debt to those who trust and follow you? Do you want colleagues to become the best they can be for the benefit of children? The suggestions offered in this chapter and the remaining chapters will provide you with plenty of opportunities to test yourself against such difficult questions. They are listed in alphabetical order so as to create a mindset, a personal framework—an approach to the job and your work every day toward the goal of being a dynamic leader. Because of the complexities and distractions in the role of school leader, one might cite survival as a mark of success and be satisfied with that accomplishment. But we know there is more, much more.

These suggestions are also direct enough to open your mind to skills and ideas you might not have thought about recently or acquired to date. They may also help you prioritize seemingly unimportant items that might have "passed you by." Children deserve nothing less than the best—a dynamic leadership and a dedicated faculty working hand in hand with committed administrators and the community to determine the destiny of a school. Net result, children win.

Ask for Frequent Feedback.

In teacher education programs, educators are taught to provide their students feedback concerning their learning in the classroom and at school. Usually, feedback should be immediate, personalized, early, and often, creating opportunities for the learner to reflect and self-adjust. While educators often disagree as to what constitutes quality feedback and what these opportunities should be, one thing is clear: whether in the classroom or outside of it, all learning requires feedback. With this feedback spirit in mind, school leaders need to stop and check how things are really going using common feedback techniques. But this is not always the case and school leaders sometimes march on.

Even well-intentioned school leaders can develop a serious condition called *cluelessness* (Bohman & Deal, 2003). You hear groups of teachers talking about some of the classic symptoms: "Well, she didn't have a clue!" (referring to the last faculty meeting when the lead teacher reacted to what teachers on her team might need to prepare for state exams) or "I didn't seem to get the memo on that." (referring to the lack of understanding by an assistant principal when teachers seem to be confused or angry over a new district policy on cheating). Other symptoms can be seen in a leader self-diagnosing an issue such as: "What went wrong with my great idea about restructuring teams?" "Why are teachers resisting?" "Why are parents concerned about the new cell phone policy?" "Don't they realize what we are dealing with!"

Cluelessness can be treated by effectively using the strategy of asking for feedback. As simple as it sounds consider asking questions, early and often, to those who are directly involved in the issues. Sample questions such as the following might be helpful: "How did you interpret that comment made by Joan at the department meeting?" "Do you think everyone feels that way?" "How do you think we are doing when it comes to meeting our goals and objectives?" "What do you think we should change?"

Whether it's a formal survey, show of hands, thumbs up, thumbs down, feedback has benefits for the leader. First, it provides clues as to how the task, issue, event, or behavior is being perceived and evaluated. For example, a teacher reading the newspaper at a faculty meeting gives the impression that the meeting is not important; a student who falls asleep during a class lecture provides as much information as the student who actively responds to the teacher's questions. Other feedback-questioning techniques can apply to faculty, students, and parents by asking questions such as: "How is that *(fill in the blank)* working out for you?" "How can I help make your work easier?"

One feedback technique used at the end of the year was to provide faculty with the opportunity to evaluate my performance as a school leader. This is not for the faint-of-heart or thin-skinned leader, but I found this feedback technique to be useful and worthwhile in setting personal and professional goals for myself.

Without feedback, school leaders can stray off course and become clueless when simple feedback techniques could assist in meaningful dialogue about what is happening in the school organization. Being a dynamic school leader means leading by being a model learner—one who consistently demonstrates what it looks like to learn and asking for clarification about his own learning through valuable and genuine feedback.

Be Wary of Your Achilles Heel.

Dynamic leaders have strengths and usually lots of them. Strong points like charisma, good listening skills, smart thinking, and complex problem solving abilities, which are keys to success; however, when one or two characteristics dominate the list beware.

Howard is a dynamic principal. He never sees himself as one because he is too busy being a servant leader. He is constantly looking for staff members to assist, children to help, and problems to solve. He enjoys problem solving, but mostly he is a "pleaser." He wants everyone to be happy.

He believes a happy teacher will be a better teacher. He believes a happy child will be a better learner. He believes a happy custodian will be a better maintenance person. He believes a happy cook will serve up better food. If he sees a child walking down the hall with a shoe untied, he will always say, "Hi and please tie your shoe." With a younger child he will even tie the shoe for the child, taking the time to chat and get to know the child better. He has a great reputation for being fair and honest, kind and considerate. Although he usually makes good decisions, on occasion he makes decisions that backfire. He makes decisions that wind up hitting him right in the face.

If a teacher is late, he will ask, "Are you OK?" If the teacher is late again he will ask, "Are you OK?" By the third time he wakes up and finally realizes there is a problem. A better adage for him would be: "Fool me once shame on you, fool me twice shame on me." Howard would be better off tempering his zealous desire to please and trust with a little dose of reality and skepticism. On the other hand, living life with a positive belief in people is so much healthier. The point here is that being pleasing, kind, and trusting are wonderful qualities to be exercised, but with a little discretion and tempering. Best to keep a little guarded and to remember that your greatest strengths can come back to haunt you.

Dynamic leaders understand that their greatest strengths can be their greatest resources but they need to realize that the flip side to those strengths can be significant deficits and problematic weaknesses.

What are your greatest strengths? More importantly, what is it about those strengths that you need to be ever cautious and guarded about, and cognizant of? If you aren't sure, just ask someone you know well and trust.

Howard's friends and relatives have given him a T-shirt that says, "Crowd Pleaser." If your strengths are noteworthy, they will stick out like a sore thumb.

Befriend the Best.

I remember my Psychology 101 class back in the fall of 1968. I listened intently as the professor discussed genetics versus environment and their effects upon us as human beings. Needless to say I was very interested. I concluded then and there that my control in life would be through my environment and most certainly not in my heredity. I was determined that I would carefully choose my collective environments and, in particular, those with whom I would associate.

The age-old debate as to whether we are shaped by heredity or environment will probably go on forever. Last time I checked, each had about equal play. I certainly cannot control what I have been given, but to an extent I can control certain aspects of my environment. Dynamic leaders know this. They know that their greatest strength can come from their association with others, from those with whom they befriend, trust, and come to call *colleague*.

Did your parents ever say, "You will be judged by the company you keep?" Don't we often caution students to pick and choose their friends wisely? Our concerns may stem from the fact that some students can be a bad influence on others. Another may stem from the group members coming together that causes undesirable things to happen. In any event, we sometimes tend to caution children about their friends, not preach and alienate, but to teach and befriend.

Have you ever said "guilty by association" to a child during an incident? I am reminded of the bully who taunts a child while the bystanders just watch. We have seen this in society during very trying times where people do nothing. Are bystanders guilty by association? Maybe not, but they are guilty of something—apathy if nothing else.

I suggest that the same general principle holds true at school. Dynamic leaders know that they can be energized and enlightened by those colleagues who care deeply about children and who are smart, hard working, sincere, and trustworthy individuals. They realize that being with the "best" provides them an avenue to think better, perform better, and live better. In short, they personally get better. I know this worked for me. I never considered myself more than just average in intellect. However, when surrounded by the best colleagues, I looked good, performed better, and was always ahead of where I would have been alone or in less-than-adequate company.

Dorothy befriends a lot of characters in the *Wizard of Oz*, all of whom were trustworthy with noble goals and kind hearts. Like Dorothy and her colleagues, if we seek intellect, heart, courage, and truth, what better way to do it than by carefully choosing our colleagues? By associating with, or hiring if the opportunity presents itself, the smartest, hardest working, most child-centered people you can find, and then allowing them to assist you, you will have gained strength and wisdom and will be known as a dynamic leader. You don't have to be in the lead with your colleagues, you just have to be in the pack.

Come to Understand Slowly— But Only if Time Permits.

An intruder enters your building and…
Two students are engaged in a fight, one with a weapon and…
The fire alarm sounds and…
A colleague is experiencing shortness of breath and…
A student is missing and…

School days can be hectic and, without question, some events require our immediate attention. There is no time to ponder the meaning of life when the tornado drill signal is blaring. You better know what to do and do it quickly. On the other hand much of what we encounter every day does permit us additional time to understand—the supreme luxury in our profession: to pause, think, and reflect. Give some thought to how you would handle the following events:

A student seems angry, disengaged, and preoccupied in class and...

A friendly colleague ignores your greeting and...

Two students seem angry with each other and...

You are told of an unplanned transfer and...

The lunch lines are too long and...

Sometimes in life it is best to come to understand slowly. If immediate action is not warranted, why not use time to your advantage. By doing so several outcomes are possible. First, the problem may just go away. This can happen with students and adults who can be "crisis junkies"—moving from one crisis to the next. Second, the problem's solution could become self-evident, with an apparent solution that keeps everybody happy. Last, the problem could continue to exist with a solution that won't come without deeper understanding.

Remember the TV show *Columbo*. Peter Falk played an annoying detective who just keeps asking questions. He is always trying to understand and find out "Who dun it?" Albeit very annoying, he solves the cases, one right after another, by carefully and meticulously seeking to understand. There it is: use time wisely—seek first to understand, not judge, and in doing so you will avoid mistakes. Mistakes such as innocently blaming a child for something you thought the child did, that the child did not do, just because it appears as though the child did, can be avoided. Or rushing to answer a child's simple question, giving a complex answer, which with further questioning could have been simply answered. Like the young child who asks, "Where do babies come from?" The parent gives a lengthy discourse on sex education only to discover that the child was looking for the word "hospital." You can also avoid embarrassing headlines like, "School Chief Gives Chase"—the story of a promising young school administrator who, upon seeing thieves stealing bicycles, hopped in his car and drove after them rather than calling the police. The police chief reprimanded him saying, "Next time please just let us do our job."

Take a lesson from the Rolling Stones: *Time is on My Side. Yes it is. Oh, yes it is.*

Dare to Be Different.

Miss or Master?

Good morning, Miss Jones. Nice work, Master Smith. Good answer, Miss Lucky.

No, these are not greetings to colleagues or people of higher authority or dignitary status. They are greetings and comments made to students. As a teacher I learned to use my English heritage early on. By employing children's last names they learned I was different, although I was doing it at the time out of pure respect. Years later, as a principal, I learned that it was unusual to call children by their last names (don't get me wrong here first names are great, last names are just not commonly used). Using last names was perceived as a form of respect and initially the surprise element made me stand out with the students. In short, the children enjoyed it, became accustomed to it, and learned to associate politeness, respect, courtesy and a little creativity with me. It was endearing.

Which Pin Should I Wear Today?

For more than two decades my wife poked fun at me in the morning as I stared at boxes of lapel pins. Which pin should I wear today? Which one made the most sense for the upcoming day? Well, it was fall, Halloween was around the corner, but Johnny likes this one, report cards are this week, student council elections are today, and so on. Nancy, my wife, only wished I were this concerned about furniture selection or painting the house. She would say, "Will you get a life?"

It all started one day by simply wearing a pin such as a flag. Then on special occasions like Valentines Day, I bought a Snoopy heart pin. Then my sister, Barbara, (you have to love those kindergarten teachers!) gave me one for St. Patrick's Day. Add pins for the seasons, the holidays, special occasions, and one day I looked and had more than 200 to choose from. Students would call me the "Pin Man" and look every day to see which one I was wearing. Even the older students enjoyed it. Children would frequently return from vacation and say, "Dr. B. I got this pin for you." It was heartwarming that they were even thinking about me. Over time pins for all occasions and from different places would find their way to me. Patriotic ones and our school mascot (the eagle) were very popular. I was different (OK, perhaps even nutty), but the pins provided an initial speaking point with children besides the morning greeting of "Good morning, Miss Smith." Students wanted to "check me out" to see what was the pin of the day.

So, what makes you stand out in a crowd?

Dare to be different. But be different in a smart way that makes you demonstrate your respect, care, and compassion, and in doing so, you will develop closer relationships with your students and colleagues.

Don't Be a One-Hit Wonder.

I remember taking a vacation with my family to the Bahamas. We were sitting by the pool and this new song kept being played over and over again. I am a real zero with my children when it comes to choosing a song that will be a hit. However, as I listened to this never-before-heard song, I kept telling them I loved it and it is going to be a hit. My children chose to simply marginalize me and not tell me I was wrong. "OK, dad," was the answer I received. After flying back home we were picked up at the airport and, sure enough, on the way home, *Who Let the Dogs Out* was playing on the radio. It became a big hit. I will never be remembered for my musical genius but, that one time, and only that one time, I was right.

Do you recall any of these ten artists? They all have something in common with Baha Men who sang *Who Let the Dogs Out.*

The Penguins (*Earth Angel*)

Frigid Pink (*House of the Rising Sun*)

Bertie Higgins (*Key Largo*)

Toni Basil (*Mickey*)

Mountain (*Mississippi Queen*)

Barry Bloom (*Montego Bay*)

Brewert Shipley (*One Toke Over the Line*)

Blue Image (*Ride Captain Ride*)

Soft Cell (*Tainted Love*)

Norman Greenbaum (*Spirit in the Sky*)

These artists were all one-hit wonders. I enjoyed all of them (I am just showing my age here and by the way welcome to my world if you recognized all of these songs, too). But they came and went. It's that simple.

As a school leader one does not want to be a one-hit wonder. Our profession does not allow us to shine in only one aspect of our leadership ability. Even if it is in a critical area like school improvement or test results, one will be long forgotten if one ignores all the other components of a successful school leader. Other arenas like student relationships, parent communications, curriculum and staff development, evaluating teaching and learning, attendance, technological literacy, and life-long learning are all areas that need to be simultaneously nurtured and developed to be a dynamic school leader.

So, develop and strengthen all your leadership skills; otherwise, you may be joining one-hit wonders and be out with the dogs.

(*Note:* The top ten list was created on April 8, 2009, choosing songs from the "One Hit-Wonder Central" website at http://www.onehitwondercentral.com/top100.cfm and from http://www.listology.com/content_show.cfm/content_id.17314.)

Engage the Broader School Community.

In the opening scene of Meredith Wilson's classic musical, *The Music Man*, a train compartment full of traveling salesmen discuss their infamous peer, "Professor Harold Hill." When one salesman speaks out about his salesmanship, another protests, "But he doesn't know the TERRITORY!"

You have to know the school territory! Oh yes you do! You have to engage businesses, agencies, organizations, churches, synagogues, and temples that comprise and serve your school community. Who is a member of the Kiwanis? Rotary? Womens' Club? Retirement center? Local Chamber of Commerce? Who represents the area in local and state government? Find out who is the city/village manager, chief of police, and the fire chief. Discover what the realtors are saying about the schools when selling property. A dynamic school leader knows the territory of neighborhood influence. As neighborhoods become increasingly complex and the school becomes the central agency for community expression, a school leader should be familiar with the leadership structure of the broader school neighborhood.

To be successful, schools require broad-based community support and that support comes from a community that is well informed, involved, and invested in its local school. These relationships do not happen overnight; they need to be facilitated and nurtured.

Unfortunately some school leaders realize all too late that their community-based school support is lacking. For instance, consider funding and referendum campaigns based on a false optimism that is crushed by the harsh reality of election day when they fail, or leaders who fall short in recognizing changing community demographics, such as vacant property giving way to subdivisions and strip malls. Then there are leaders who don't understand intense opposition to a proposed boundary change. In these instances, school leaders hear a myriad of complaints as concerned citizens file into a school board meeting and fill the room from wall to wall. It is too late to begin mending fences and informing the community about school issues when individuals are upset and angry.

In an era of communities wanting educators to do more with less, a dynamic leader takes the time to develop a positive school image by providing frequent, accurate, and honest information, by listening to all sides of an issue, and by developing plans of action so as to gather data, thus building relationships and engaging the school's broader-based constituency.

Fine-Tune Your Acting Abilities.

Some say the school can be viewed as a stage—even a theatre if you will—where the actors and actresses are parents, teachers, administrators, and students playing out assigned roles within any school day. The activities or performances that engage these actors and actresses might be as common as an irate parent wanting a change in a bus stop for their child and expressing it loudly to whomever will listen or the discipline of students in a lunch line waiting to get their food. Picture the drama in these possible school plays and imagine the role of the school leader. *Guess Who's Coming to Dinner?* (or to your classroom or meeting), *The Time of Our Life* (in detention, or at the dance), *Our Town* (when trying to pass a referendum or creating a strategic plan), *All's Well That Ends Well* (after trying to settle a conflict between two teachers, two parents or students) or *They're Playing Our Song* (when test scores go up). Certainly the school leader has been given a major role in these new, inventive scripts.

Faculty meetings can be wonderful examples of settings in which educators engage in dramatic performances. Who was at the meeting? Who left early? Who came late? What issues were brought forward? What solutions were given? What emotional performances were heard in order to get a point across? What did the leader do or not do? What are the next steps? Some meetings attract more performers and larger audiences, such as school board meetings concerned with hiring personnel, expelling students, or restructuring the school. These occasions bring out collective drama as parent actors ban together to make sure issues get more attention. One can quickly see the role of the school leader become more intense, complex, and thorny.

Recognize these theatrics and muster the opportunity to guide the school actors and actresses in a positive way. For example do your words complement your body language? Are you so relaxed that no one takes you seriously when you say, "But, there really is no more money left in the budget"? Or can you clench your fists and stiffen your muscles to show your exasperation at the fact that this year's monies are truly gone? Can you demonstrate intensity and passion in your voice for an emotional cause, such as a student who is in desperate need of social work services? Are your gestures in check so that when you look in a certain way or move in a certain way it has purpose and meaning? The nature of the professional actor who conveys his or her feelings on the stage can serve as an example of skills to be mastered by the school leader.

Remember some colleagues are listening and watching your messages through emotions such as delight, apprehension, fear, hope, doubt, and panic. These feelings are their sense of reality. Other individuals will be watching and listening through sequential, clear actions such as Step #1, How? Step #2, When? Step #3, Who? Step #4, Where? This is their sense of reality. The delivery of lines from the school leader should evoke clarity, confidence, and trust—not confusion, bewilderment, and uncertainty. Actors and actresses are influenced by the roles they play, which in turn affect their daily lives. Will those who know you respond to your role with, "BRAVO! BRAVO!"?

Foster Purposeful and Consistent Communication.

Please pass me a napkin so I can write that down. Thanks for the scrap of paper from the recycle bin; I can take ten notes on this piece of paper. Here is a note for you.

Am I crazy or just communicative? Probably both.

As a teacher I was always writing things down so as not to forget something. I would even keep paper and a pencil under my bed to write down ideas that came to me in the middle of the night. Ideas for a lesson or a way to help a child can come at any time. How will you remember them?

As a principal I was constantly taking notes about "things"—"things" teachers needed; "things" that would make for a better life for students; "things" that needed to be repaired; "things" that needed to be ordered; and "things" that mattered to people even if they seemed relatively insignificant to me at the time. Most importantly, it was "things" to make the school a better place for children and "things" that mattered to people that I did not want to forget. At the end of the day, I would empty my pockets and have a collage of paper that gave me a roadmap to make the school better. If really important and time sensitive I tended to keep the note in my hand. Likewise if I were writing a note to someone I would write it on a corner of a piece of paper or some paper item that was small and about to be discarded. People came to learn my style and knew that if I wrote something down they told me, or if I passed them a note on a scribbled piece of paper, it was important. We would usually remember the content of the information, even if we lost the paper. Partly because the communication system became a humorous point of conversation, but mostly because they knew I cared and that if I took the time to pass a message on, or take one down, it was important. Most "things" are rarely earth shattering but resolved "things" do make the school a better place. I could have kept a small notepad in my pocket (which is what I recommend); however, necessity is the mother of invention and when I was without paper a few times I noticed people would laugh and say, "I bet we can give him five notes from that candy bar wrapper." Or, upon receiving a note a teacher would say, "Do you really expect me to remember what is on this tiny piece of paper?" Well, guess what—the teacher did!

    I have always said that it is frequently the mosquitoes in life that bother us. It is those small pesky things, like classrooms that are too cold or too hot; materials that were borrowed, not returned, and needed for a lesson; a broken piece of equipment; the garbage can that does not get emptied; your missing yogurt from the refrigerator; the broken door lock; a colleague's insult; the nasty parent call (add your list here please) that bother us. Unlike mosquito bites that when left untouched usually go away, these items don't fix themselves. They don't go away and frequently fester to create bigger problems.

    Sometimes things can't be fixed either because the money is not there or it is just not in the cards, but frequently the small "things" can be attended to: the lock can be fixed, the garbage can be emptied, unhappy parents can be addressed and materials can be found. Dynamic leaders care, communicate and constantly and consistently collect information to make schools a better place for everyone. By promoting, encouraging, fostering, and creating two-way consistent and purposeful communication, you say to people you care about them and the children, and you will do the best you can to make things better.

Know Everyone's Name and Then Some.

George, a student in my graduate class, asked me about knowing the names of the students in an entire high school. I had mentioned in class that it took me about six weeks after school started to learn every student and employee name in a school of 500 children. "Oh, he said, that's because it was an elementary school." He thought that it would be impossible in a large high school. Why would a school leader want to do this? My answer was, "Why not!"

Knowing a person's name shows familiarity, friendship, and attention to detail. It says from the other hundreds of people who are in a school, I know you and can separate you from the rest. Some student names are quickly learned like those who are in trouble, high achievers or those individuals who have a way of crossing your path everywhere you go. If you know everyone's name you can even graduate to a higher rung of the ladder and then some by knowing the names of other members of the family like an employee's spouse or children or in the case of a student, his or her siblings. What you are creating is a portrait of interest—I know you; I am interested in you—and this picture has depth and texture.

Of course knowing everyone's name is not done overnight. Dynamic leaders know that the effort is worth the time. They decide that they want to remember a name and begin focusing and organizing information that will help them remember. They might use a mnemonic or association technique like: Blue eyes = Blake, Fun = Florina, and Zip = Zipporah. Leaders learn names over time but do so systematically and deliberately. They may attempt to learn about a dozen new names each day. They reject the old phrase, "Well, I am not very good with names so I won't bother."

At my local grocery store the cashier calls me by my name and I call her by her name. She is wearing a name tag so it is easy for me to remember her name, but she has remembered my name for years now—tough job considering the hundreds of customers who check out their groceries with her every day. It makes me feel good. When I am in the grocery store I look for her and if she is there, I quickly move my cart into her check out line because she is friendly, polite, and pleasant.

Knowing everyone's name in a school will pay dividends and bonuses in your quest to become a dynamic school leader. For example, in my case, it would come back to me that parents in the neighborhood would be talking about school and someone would state the fact that I knew every child's name before parent-teacher conferences. When parents would call with a concern, I could say, "Oh yes, I saw Bill today and he was working hard on his citizenship project." The fact that I knew the child and his name created common ground to begin our conversation without confrontation. My supervisor even put on my evaluation, "And by the way she knows everybody's name in the school and then some...."

Mind Your Mouth.

"You say that again and I will wash your mouth out with soap." While I am sure that never happened to you, just the thought of that bar of Ivory Soap (or Lava Soap if you can remember the brand with volcanic pumice) swirling around in my mouth was really nauseating. Although poor language does need to be "cleaned up," it may be worth considering a "clean up" for the incredibly stupid, naïve, distasteful, boring, worthless, hurting, and critical statements that can find their way into daily conversations. Our colleagues' memories tend to be long on conversations heard that are negative. Abraham Lincoln said, "Better to remain silent and be thought a fool than to speak out and remove all doubt" (http://www.timelinequotes.com/author/Abraham_Lincoln.html).

These are truly words of wisdom. I worked with a teacher for three decades who would take everything in at a team meeting then speak only a few words, softly, near the end. By that time he looked the smartest, had concluded the best course of action, and maintained everyone's respect. Ron was very effective in team meetings because he carefully listened to everyone's point of view and position on a topic. He was very opinionated, but sound logic would cause him to change his position, or, if needed, "take one for the team." He always acted in what he believed was in the students' best interest. Much of what we do in education can be judgmental and by listening first, you earn people's respect and gain their ear.

My dad used to say some people just like to hear themselves talk. This can be so true. Ever have the conversation that lasted for minutes and found yourself daydreaming only to catch yourself somewhere in the middle of the conversation. Then you repeat something the person said so the person really thinks you heard the whole thing. By the way that is a good technique in case you have not used it. But the point here is what do you want people to think about *you*. What do you want them to remember at the end of the day? If you want to be a dynamic leader take the advice our mothers told us when we were young: "God gave us two ears and one mouth so that we will listen twice as much as we speak." And while you are listening, listen carefully with your eyes focused and your mind cleared, move closer, and demonstrate you care. Each and every conversation is a relationship building block.

Leaders build on relationships, cultivate them, and do so by watching what comes out of their mouth. Mind your mouth and you will be seen as a careful listener and a potential contributor.

Prioritize Using the Three "P" Philosophy.

"Howard, would you mind watching my class for me. I have to go to the washroom. I know the schedule will be changed next year, but four classes in a row are too many. I do not even have enough time to go to the bathroom."

"Of course I will and I do apologize again for the awful schedule. It will be fixed next year."

If it's not a challenging schedule then it will just be something else. The day is filled with problems, concerns, events, surprises, complaints, reports, committees, meetings, comments, situations, questions, and, unfortunately, emergencies. As Mary, a superior teacher, used to tell me, "Oh, yeah, and on occasion we even teach!" She used to chuckle and follow that up with, "See you later, Howard. I think I will go do that part-time job now."

So how does one navigate those daily events and remain sane? How does one do the best one can and still find time to go to the washroom? The answer lies in prioritizing your actions, of course dealing with emergencies first, and then following the *Three "P"* prioritization philosophy.

The first "P" is *people* and it is all about relationships. With all the choices one has to make in a day, take care of people and, of course, children before anything else. Great schools can be defined by the relationships that exist between and among all the players. You can "feel" it when you walk in a school where people care about each other. It all starts with putting people where they belong—with you in building those relationships.

The second "P" is *phones* and emails which require a significant amount of time when done right. Those phone calls and emails, many of which require a response, can really pile up. In today's world of technology, it seems you can always be found. After taking care of people, finish up those phone calls and emails.

The third "P" represents the *papers* to be graded, reports to be completed, articles and books to be read, and a whole host of "pulp-like products" to grapple with. And we are not talking *Pulp Fiction* here but real pulp. But, alas, something has to be last. Something has to get the low priority, and suffice it to say, it is paper, which includes all those items requiring your reading, many of which are now on the Internet. You have to get to them, but they definitely come after people and phones.

So, there you have it. Prioritize your actions by using the following *Three "P"* prioritization policy: *People, Phones,* and *Paper.*

Reach Out to Uninvolved Parents.

No, I can't come to school because…

> I don't have a babysitter.
>
> I don't speak English.
>
> I work two jobs.
>
> I don't have a car.
>
> All I ever hear is "bad news" when I come.
>
> We don't have a computer at home.
>
> I didn't get the paper about school events. Was it sent home?
>
> I am too busy.
>
> I didn't have a good school experience and don't like going to school.

Parents who don't show up for conferences, appointments, or report card pickups can be upsetting to school leaders. Notes sent home without responses, permission slips left unsigned, and no telephone at home can be perceived as a lack of interest in a student's education.

Reach out but don't blame parents and guardians who appear to be invisible when it comes to school. Don't perpetuate an out-of-date stereotype that if parents don't come to school, they don't care about their children. It is typical of parents and caregivers in poverty schools to feel that they are already failing to raise their children properly. To emphasize this feeling by creating a feeling of inferiority, mistrust, and disrespect in the home–school relationship makes little sense.

Dynamic leaders are proactive and have exceptional parent relationship skills. They view uninvolved parents as partners, not inferiors, and continue to search for the right occasion to bring them to school. If you have parents and guardians who are not coming to school, here are some ideas to think about:

1. Explore your own attitude about uninvolved parents. Are some parents from different cultures and hold different values about schooling compared to the mainstream parents? Do you hold any stereotypes that may be communicated unconsciously?

2. Establish a rapport with families before problems arise. For example, you might contact a reclusive parent or caregiver to ask about what school goals they have for their child as the school year begins. You might be able to have an early conference.

3. Make flexible meeting times for working parents. This demonstrates the school's willingness to accommodate them. Saturday mornings and evening meetings could work well. Providing child care and interpreters is appealing to all in attendance.

4. Keep inviting parents to school. Just like a broken record invite them to coffees, family nights, parent discussion groups, concerts, plays, guest speakers, and athletic events.

5. In larger schools keep in touch with school counselors and social workers about parents of concern. Make home visits if necessary.

The purpose of having *all* parents come to school is to learn more about their children.

Don't take "no" for an answer. Find the key to unlock uninvolved parents and learn how to develop a positive, involved relationship with them.

Seize the Lead in Challenging Times.

Picture this:

You are the principal of a building and having an instrumental concert tonight. The students are excited, arrive early, and are ready to end the day on a high note (a little humor here). They run into your office twenty minutes before the concert is to begin with excitement in their voices and jumping up and down for joy. They tell you that a major TV station has arrived for the concert. A cameraman and a famous news reporter are on their way up the walkway. The children are sooooo excited, so pumped and ready to play. Intuitively you know that the reporter has not come for a concert. You learn that the reporter is there to interview *you* and ask *you* about a testing "irregularity" (that is what the state board ultimately called it; the reporter would call it a scandal) that has occurred with students' answers being changed on a high-stakes state test. So, what do you do?

A. Hide behind the stage and listen to the concert.

B. Disguise yourself as a student and learn to play the flute.

C. Find the closest bathroom.

D. Sneak out the back door and go home.

Obviously, the answer is "none of the above." Dynamic leaders understand the classic comment: "When the going gets tough, the tough get going." They understand that during the most challenging of times they must step forward, separate themselves from their colleagues, and be the leader. The principal in the aforementioned predicament should meet with the press, meet with the parents, meet with the students, meet with his superintendent, and ultimately create a plan for managing the situation.

Dynamic leaders seize the lead. They run point the same way a platoon designates a specific person to "run point," to lead the patrol, or a basketball team has a point guard to lead the offense. It may be the most uncomfortable day of your life, but it is your responsibility to lead the way. When the alarms go off, a child endangers himself, the school floods, inclement weather sets in during dismissal, or there is that bad accident, dynamic leaders "run point" and know that their reputation will long be remembered by what they do and how well they respond. Placing children first, being concerned for safety, being calm, cool, and collected are all variables that will be replayed during and after the event. And, in any event, that is how you will be evaluated and remembered. There are no second chances here.

Dynamic leaders take charge, take responsibility, and "run the show" during tough times. They don't pass the buck. They "run point" and seize the lead.

Take a Lickin' and Keep on Tickin'.

"You should be fired."

I remember the words like they were yesterday, although it was more than two decades ago. The man, who towered over me, looked down, with anger in his voice, and told me with crystal clarity as he left the building exactly what he thought of me. There was absolutely no room for doubt. I should be history.

It was a 7:00 PM on a fairly cool but nice November evening. The school was having its traditional concert to support the book fair. Historically, the concert lasted for thirty minutes, providing significant time for parents to attend the annual book fair with their children. The book fair was a good fundraiser (as parents bought holiday book presents in addition to books for themselves and their children; it was a good educational event with a fine arts promotion). The problem was that the concert went on for two hours. The traditional choral concert theme was changed to a talent show. The music teacher and I thought it was a great opportunity to showcase talent, and we did not want to leave anyone out. Sort of a "No Talent Left Behind Show." Although *every cow is sacred to its mother* (Paul Houston, AASA), most were upset that night. The show ended about the same time the book fair was supposed to end and everyone should have gone home. There was little time to buy books. Most people were polite but very upset. Some were angry. So what did I do? It would have been easy to sneak out the back door, but not the right thing to do. I stood by the exit and greeted everybody as they left. I was pouring sweat, listening to all the criticisms and taking 100% of the heat. I apologized profusely, said I had learned a lesson, and smiled a lot. Yes, smiled (as best I could). "Have a good evening," was muttered constantly (I knew I wouldn't).

There are numerous events in teachers' and administrators' lives where people get upset and sometimes downright angry. Parents, colleagues, and community members can get upset over lots of things. The poor report card grade that "the teacher gave"; the social situation that the school created; the teasing that "everyone has been oblivious about"; the child who did not make the team who should have; the class list that was so "poorly planned"; the "stupid" rules that have to be followed; the ridiculous start time (or end time, just pick one) of the school day; the poor bus routing; the unhealthy (or too healthy) food in the cafeteria; and, of course, too much homework (or not enough—my favorite is when you get two calls in the same day saying directly opposite things on the same situation).

So what do dynamic leaders do? How do they take the heat? Here are some guidelines:

1. Be professional and do not add to the problem (who is right or wrong is wholly irrelevant).

2. Smile.

3. Look the person (or persons) in the eyes.

4. Take one step closer.

5. Restate the concern.

6. Listen attentively and don't interrupt.

7. Respond to the concern as best you can (at all times trying to put children first; e.g., in the situation above, we were trying to include all the children in the program).

8. Apologize if the situation warrants it or at least acknowledge their concern is legitimate to the person complaining.

9. Take notes (it is always good to keep Post-its and a pen/pencil on you).

10. And, if appropriate, call the person in a couple days (time usually slows the anger process) and report on the situation.

It never bothered me that people likened me to a "Bozo the Clown" punching bag. Remember those blowup life-size figurines that when you hit them they would just come right back up. You might not enjoy the hit but if you don't take it personally, it helps. Dynamic leaders smile and take one step forward. They listen; they care; and then they respond. They don't aggravate the problem. *And then they move on to the next problem at hand.* Like the Timex watch commercials used to say, "take a lickin' and keep on tickin'."

Take Rumor and Hearsay in Stride.

Time: 8:30 AM

Date: Monday morning

Location: Pleasant High School—Room #44

Teacher: Miss Match

Reputation: Superior

Miss Match:

"Good morning class. I hope you all had a wonderful weekend. What are some things you did this weekend?...OK, that sounds good...OK....Oh, thank you for asking how my weekend was. I had a very good weekend although I think I may be coming down with a cold. I am not feeling 100% today....Does anyone know why your classmate, John, is not here? Oh, he's running late because he had to help his little sister who broke her arm at the hospital. I am sorry to hear that. Thank you. Let's start today's lesson on exponents."

Time: 9:15 AM

Date: Same Day

Location: Pleasant High School Hallway—passing time

Two Students (girls) Chatting:

"Hey did John get to school yet? He did, good. I need to talk to him. Our turnabout dance is coming up in a few weeks, and I am going to ask him to go with me. You know, I really like Miss Match; she is an excellent algebra teacher. She cares about her students. It was really nice of her to ask about John. I hope his sister will be fine. I heard she may need surgery for her arm"

Time: Noon

Date: Same Day

Location: Lunchroom

A Random Student Chatting in the Lunchroom:

"Hey, did you hear that Miss Match had surgery over the weekend for her arm?"

Time: 6:00 PM

Date: Same Day

Location: A student's home (dinnertime)

Parent: "So how was school today?"

Student: "Fine."

Parent: So, what did you do?"

Student: "Nothing."

Parent: "Anything new."

Student: "Oh, yeah. Miss Match went to the hospital for a broken arm."

Remember the game "telephone." Everyone sits in a circle and one person whispers a sentence into the ear of the person next to him. Then everyone takes turns passing that sentence along, whispering it into the ear of the next person. By the time it gets to the last person, who says the sentence out loud, it is frequently different—sometimes completely different. School life can be just like the game of "telephone." Thousands of conversations are transferred daily among students, faculty, and parents. And many of them get unintentionally twisted and turned by virtue of being passed on, the passing of time and honest listening errors. And before you know it, there are "real stories" to be heard—I mean juicy ones that can just knock your socks off. Ones that really catch your attention, wake you up, are not forgotten, and you want to pass on, too. And wait—by the end of the week, these stories are headline news. Simply put, take what you hear in stride, search out the truth, and be careful what you, yourself, say. Broken arms are not the end of the world but broken reputations can be very difficult to repair.

Think Beyond Today.

Schools are living places with the constant humdrum of activities. As educators we are continuously being pulled in multiple directions and assisting students is at the forefront of any dynamic leader's list. How can anyone find time to plan for the future while trying to survive the present? Well one thing is certain—you had best plan for the future if you plan on having one.

Aesop's fable, *The Ant and the Grasshopper*, reminds us of the grasshopper who, during the warm weather, spent his time singing while the ant spent his time working to store up food for the winter. When the winter came the grasshopper found himself a day late and a dollar short. Working hard is not the issue for dynamic leaders. We all work hard. Planning for the future is what can catch us off guard. And like the grasshopper we don't want to get caught short. Consider the U.S. history teacher who has not prepared her students for state tests, the history instructor who only gets to the Vietnam War at the end of the year, and the school administrator who is not prepared for an increase in student enrollment or changing demographics. Children are the ones who pay the price for educators' poor planning.

Live the day and enjoy it. Catch your breath. But your long-term survival may depend on your ability to take the time to ponder variables such as your next curriculum innovation, technology change, new teaching strategy, or even the restructuring of that space you have been living in. I am reminded of those middle school students who begin to learn the value of and process for planning long-range assignments, such as projects due in two weeks. It can be a real challenge to learn that skill, but we know that it is one that must be mastered.

One suggestion that I found useful is to spend time on Sunday night, before that school week gets hectic, and get organized for the week. Set your goals and decide exactly what needs to be accomplished. Where can you find time to think about and plan for the future? Look at the short- and long-term needs of the week ahead of you. Think about the week but also where you want to be in three months, six months, and nine months, then let the week unfold like a story.

Some say life is too short, so just enjoy today. Others say be prepared.

Alfred E. Newman *(Mad Magazine)* says, "What, me worry?" Well, dynamic leaders think beyond today. They worry about the future and plan carefully for it. They know that planning for the future virtually guarantees that it will be a brighter one.

Treasure School Rituals, Ceremonies, and Traditions.

What do graduations, open houses, faculty meetings, field days, homecoming, field trips, proms, and retirement dinners (just to mention a few) have in common? Similar to families looking forward to annual vacations or celebrating birthdays and anniversaries, they are recurring events. On the surface these events may appear mundane; however, in reality these events communicate a much deeper meaning of spirit and passion for home and school.

As I see it, examples of school rituals could be registering for school, buying school supplies from a list, welcoming speeches, pep rallies, and electing a homecoming queen or king. Ceremonies could be large, gala events that mark milestones, such as retirement dinners, homecoming festivities, and proms. Traditions can become ritualistic and ceremonial, such as a graduation. At first glance a novice leader may perceive these events as unnecessary and time-consuming. For example, as a new principal I thought a kindergarten graduation and ceremony were a little peculiar. Isn't graduation a culminating experience? Caps and gowns for five-year-olds? How can kindergartners who have twelve more years of schooling be finishing their education? I soon discovered through conversations that this ceremony was a tradition with history and significance in the school and no parent of a kindergartner wanted their child to miss their "moment in the sun" at the end of their kindergarten year. So should this ceremony be continued?

Here is an opportunity for a dynamic school leader to negotiate the meaning of graduation with kindergarten teachers, parents, and students. Why are we holding on to this graduation ceremony? What does it mean for us as a school? Certainly there are rituals, ceremonies, and traditions that have outlived their usefulness and should be abandoned, but this was not one of them.

Dynamic school leaders are sensitive to the school's history, culture, traditions, ceremonies, and rituals. In fact, they build on them. They seek to use the school's observances as ways to emphasize the uniqueness of the school and what everyone values. These events can clarify values, bond individuals, and inspire reflection and insights about accomplishments.

A school's history does not start when *you* walk into the building. Much has already happened and others have gone before you (even in a brand new school). Should you misread, misunderstand, or disregard school rituals, ceremonial opportunities, and traditions, you might alienate many school stakeholders and be perceived as cold and insensitive. Conversely, as a dynamic leader you have the opportunity to build upon, cherish, treasure, and/or even create new rituals, ceremonies, and traditions in your stead.

Tune into the Politics.

I went to the inauguration dinner of our university's new president. It was a wonderful occasion, the end of a week of festivities. Being one of the "new kids on the block," I thought it would be a good idea to attend. My colleagues were surprised to find me seated with the president's family and friends. They thought I must be a person of influence. How was it? What did you learn? I was asked later. Did you put in a good word for us? Who do you know? It was a wonderful event, and the people were so pleasant. Was I a person of influence?

No way! My reservation got lost so I waited with the hostess until everyone was seated. She gave me the only seat left. I felt lucky, but also nervous. Why? Really, why should I be? Why were people asking me questions? Why was I nervous? It's the politics of the situation. Has the following thought ever crossed your mind "I just want to be a good teacher—why can't I just teach?"

Have you ever been asked questions such as?

Do you know you have the PTA president's daughter in your class?

Did you realize the Board President's daughter is on your team?

Are you nervous about the village manager visiting our school tomorrow?

Are you attending our school's annual fundraiser this year?

Did you sponsor the principal's son on his walkathon?

Did you buy any of that expensive candy from our department chair's daughter?

Unfortunately, sometimes being book smart and/or good in the classroom only gets you so far. Like it or not there are politics in education and dynamic leaders understand that. They understand the politics of their school and how to manage them. They don't necessarily "suck up," but they do realize, conceptualize, compartmentalize, rationalize, and ultimately cope with the politics of daily life in schools. And they do it with a smile. Dynamic leaders understand phrases like "quid pro quo" and "you scratch my back and I'll scratch yours." But it is an "understanding" and not a desire for a balance of power or influence. They "get it" and "deal with it" but in doing so they put children first. People can argue with you on your opinion but not your character when you put children first.

Dynamic leaders are sensitive to and thus react accordingly to the politics of their schools while simultaneously retaining the ability to put children first. As a matter of fact it is this ability to do both at the same time that one gets the reputation of being a political genius *and* a child advocate. So be political and understand the nuances of where you work. Roll out the red carpet for that special visitor. Give people that special attention. Know everybody's name before you meet them. Smile when you are really thinking something else. Buy that box of candy. Sponsor that walk. Greet the village official. In doing so, you will be politically smart, a child advocate, and lay the foundation for a better tomorrow. You won't have to worry about being the brunt of that old joke: "You can tell when a politician is lying—his lips move." Tune into the politics just like you would tune into a radio station—with crystal clarity.

And by the way, as with the inauguration dinner, it is sometimes better to be lucky than smart or political!

Value Parents as Allies.

At a school where I worked we would say, "Students are great if they just didn't have parents." What we all were bemoaning was the time it took away from teaching to work with parents of the students in our school. In many cases, the time spent with parents was more than the time spent with students. For example, there were parents who asked for a daily update (phone call/email/written note) as to how their child did on his or her homework. Then there were the parents who wanted to know if the weekend neighborhood fight carried over to school and could you keep track of the individuals involved and report back.

What are your school's parent involvement practices? Too much involvement? Not enough?

Many parents want to serve their school in more than a fundraising capacity or as field-trip chaperons. They might be interested in sitting on a curriculum committee to provide a parent's perspective of the content being included in a certain discipline or grade level. They might be interested in developing pupil progress reporting forms and the procedures to distribute them. Ultimately, they might want to serve on the school board or local school council. To what degree are *you* willing to have parents participate in their school?

Dynamic leaders know how to attract parents to school on a regular basis. They provide a range of meaningful parent involvement activities so as to bring parents to school and clarify parent roles and responsibilities in each activity. They monitor the activities to ensure appeal to diverse parent interests. Dynamic leaders reach out to community organizations and religious groups who serve the families of the children enrolled in the school to support and pinpoint their common needs. They are aware of the overwhelming research that links parent involvement in school with student achievement and learning.

Dust off and roll out the welcome mat for parents. Welcome parents into the school on a daily basis as observers, volunteers, and resources. Plan educational activities for parents that enable them to work with their child at home. Parent University and adult education classes can educate and support parents as they migrate issues such as homework, socialization, technology, networking, grades, health, safety and security, and even the college application process.

All too often we remember the parents who avoid us, mettle, threaten, complain, or grumble, and forget the parents who become involved and make significant contributions to the school. Building relationships with parents can yield tremendous benefits, such as higher student achievement, better attitudes toward school, and increased self-concept. In addition, parents are serving as service role models for their children. The vast majority of parents who become involved in school become wonderful allies. The home–school relationships that are built serve children and the schools for a long time after the families move on. It seems like the few parents who drive educators crazy are the ones who give other parents a bad name.

Pests or partners? Allies or adversaries? Turning parents into allies does not take a magic wand or a leadership miracle. What it does take is a dynamic leader's vision of engaging parents to take an active role and become an ally in their child's education.

2

On Becoming a Moral and Ethical Leader

Every successful school needs moral and ethical leaders. Moral leaders engender trust and trust is the key component to successful relationships whether they are at home or at work. If you ask educators why they respect certain school leaders, usually they say it is because "I trust them" or "They're trustworthy." Therefore, school leaders are seen as both demonstrating trust and fostering trusting relationships within the school. It's as easy as saying, "If you don't trust people, they won't trust you." This simple saying may appear obvious but it implies a deliberate long-term process of relationship building, caring, and consistency.

The virtuous leader in a school is one who embodies the knowledge of what is right and what is wrong. A moral leader is the person a faculty member will look up to as an example when making the right decisions and judgments. There is no room for error in schools when it comes to ethical decisions because these decisions are made in absolutes. They are moral or immoral, ethical or unethical, virtuous or sinful. Ultimately, the decisions filter through the organization and eventually reach the classroom and children.

Above all else a leader must be beyond reproach. From time to time you may make a mistake, for which absolution is given, but there is no room for error when it comes to making a moral mistake. For example, President Clinton damaged his presidency by his immoral actions in the Monica Lewinsky scandal. Examples of moral failure in schools include teachers having sex with students, principals stealing money from various school funds, and superintendents accepting gifts that violate gift ban acts. These acts have major consequences; other, less-significant failures still have consequences by impacting one's ability to be an effective leader.

Ethical educators practice what they preach and establish a moral purpose to their school (Fullan, 2003). This moral purpose is based on a belief system and a personal framework that supports educators in discovering meaning and purpose in their lives. It also impacts their day-to-day decision making by providing a "conscience" or moral lens through which decisions are made. People say "actions speak louder than words," but in reality actions *are* the words that preach the moral doctrine in each and every school demonstrated by the leader.

How should school leaders make moral and ethical decisions? The best way to start is by applying your own moral and ethical litmus test to the situation at hand. How will my decision be perceived by others? Would I want this to happen to me? Would my parents be proud of me? Do I really feel good about this?

Professional codes of ethics are embedded in virtually every educational organization, including organizations such as the American Association of School Administrators (AASA), American Federation of Teachers (AFT), and the National Education Association (NEA). Theses codes of ethics promote integrity, fairness, and ethical behavior on the part of all educators.

Another way to view moral and ethical decision making is to understand that school leaders need to find the balance between the rights of the individual and the needs of the community. For example a school leader might be engrossed in raising the test scores in his or her classroom, department, or school while overlooking individual students who might not be performing well. Another example might be a discipline case where a child commits an act for which the child can be suspended, but the school leader believes the child would not benefit from a suspension and that the suspension might even be counterproductive. But fair and equal application of school policy requires the suspension. Parents want consistency, consequences, and convictions for children who violate school rules, but the perpetrator's parents want compassion and clemency for their child. The following moral dilemma unfolds; the leader is responsible for implementing school policy and "doling out" consequences versus the leader's own sense of what the right thing to do is. So what is a leader to do? Kowalski (2004) reminds us of this duality by saying, "Treating everyone the same does not necessarily translate into treating everyone fairly."

Rosborg, McGee, and Burgett (2003) provide a hierarchical framework in the form of questions to ask oneself when reviewing moral decision making. They conclude that one needs to ask five questions when reflecting on a moral and ethical problem such as the situational examples described above. The questions to ask are:

1. Is it legal?
2. Will this decision/act follow our policies or rules?
3. Would I feel good if my family knew about it?
4. Will this decision make me proud?
5. Would I like this decision if it were done to me?

School leaders need the time to reflect and develop their own personalized code of ethics based upon their life stories, professional experiences, and moral and ethical values. Understanding oneself and reflecting on experiences can provide a process for better decision making, which benefits everyone in the end.

What causes school leaders to make unethical decisions? One reason for an ethical leadership failure could be the tendency to become caught in competing political interests. The school leader is expected to represent the interests of the community and at the same time maintain positive relationships with colleagues and students. At times these two arenas can be viewed as having opposing interests causing the leader to appear untrustworthy and unethical when in reality, the individual is trying to please everyone. For example, a school leader might "go to bat" for an excellent support staff member who deserves significantly more than a cost-of-living raise; however, the community expectation does not allow for raises beyond annual cost-of-living increases.

Overload is another cause for moral failure. With national and state pressures for school leaders to raise student achievement as well as to meet students' day-to-day needs, a school leader may resort to "fudging" test score data (more commonly known to children as cheating) to relieve the pressure to increase test scores. This error in judgment is a serious mistake, which can lead to our profession being disgraced.

What do you believe are the fundamentals necessary for moral and ethical leadership? Would you know an ethical leader if you saw one? Do you owe a professional debt to your moral hero? Do you have a professional responsibility to those who view you as their moral and ethical leader? The suggestions offered in this chapter provide you with plenty of opportunities to reflect on complex moral and ethical questions in school leadership. Again they are listed in alphabetical order to create a mind set, a personal framework for the development of a personal code of ethics—an approach to life and your work every day.

Answer to Yourself First.

Remember the queen in Walt Disney's *Sleeping Beauty* who asks: "Mirror, mirror on the wall, who's the fairest of them all."

As the wicked queen in *Snow White* frequently pondered her appearance, we should be pondering our appearance, that is, whether or not others see us as being morally and ethically fair or in balance. And while the last thing you are probably thinking about when you get up in the morning or go to bed at night is whether or not you are an example of a moral and ethical leader for all those who surround you on a daily basis, it should be. Reflecting on moral and ethical decision making starts with and ends with those daily rituals like brushing and flossing your teeth. It begins and ends with that glance in the mirror to make sure you look OK and are ready to begin the day's common routines. However, the next time you look in the mirror, take a closer look—not at the face you see but the face others see as your character. Look through the mirror and ask yourself whether or not that face you see has the quality, caring character of all those looking at you on the other side. Like a one-way mirror in a police station, if you were on the other side looking in, would you respect what you saw and, more importantly, would you view yourself as an example of ethical impeccability.

Introspection sometimes occurs best when you put a face on it. The face of moral introspection has to be your own. We all answer to ourselves first and in doing so have to live with that which we know to be true. The daily pressures in the workforce can easily cause us to sway a bit from that which we know to be just and right. Ultimately, like an out-of-body experience, we have to conclude whether or not our actions speak to the character that our profession warrants and requires. We must be objective when we judge our own behaviors. While we all have someone that holds us accountable for our ability to perform, absolute accountability in the realm of moral and ethical leadership lies with you—and only you. Next time you look in the mirror ask yourself, "Am I who I should be?" Answer candidly, reflect, and then decide whether or not you are the best example for our children and all those who proudly serve our profession.

Care Deeply.

Caring, truly caring, starts with a commitment to humanity and extends to everyone with whom you associate. The following is a true story about caring, patriotism, and civic duty.

On caring...

It was late at night—one of those cold and dreary fall days—when the phone rang.

"Hey, dad. I hope everything is fine at home. Everything is great here at Indiana University. Don't worry I have a B average. It's good that I am finishing my junior year a semester early. By the way, when you have a minute tomorrow, I need you to mail my high school diploma, Social Security card, birth certificate, and passport to me."

I'm thinking that my son has applied for an overseas college program, and it is good that he is a semester ahead of himself—an opportunity to study abroad and learn another culture and obtain a few extra semester hours of business school credit. It would be a great experience. My only thought is, "How much is this going to cost?"

"Dad, I have decided to join the Marines. It's the Marine Reserves for now. I have been thinking about this for a long time. The Reserves are my best option until I finish school. I will be going to San Diego right after Christmas through March. Then I will spend April and May in the School of Infantry as this is my MOS (military occupational specialty). Because of my test scores, they wanted me to accept a different MOS. I had a really hard time getting them to accept me into Infantry School. But, ultimately, my determination won out. They knew I meant it. Don't worry, dad, I will be going back to college to finish my senior year next September, if my reserve unit does not get called up. By the way, I hate to ask, but I need that rent money, too."

Maybe I shouldt have allowed my son to play with those toy guns when he was young? Maybe I permitted too many of those Nintendo games? Wasn't it just yesterday that he was giving the high school commencement speech? *What happened?* Was I a good father? Who knows, maybe I was better than I thought. At least I respected him enough to support the decision he had made on his own. I was so proud and so worried at the same time.

As educators we should be passionate in school to instill in our students a set of core values and beliefs. This includes, besides academics, a sense of civic duty, courage, and commitment. We know we influence our children at school far more by our actions than by the words of wisdom we so often try to impart.

One virtue moral and ethical leaders must embody if they are to lead is caring. If one truly cares, then it will be reflected in all one does. You can't demonstrate this virtue halfheartedly. Caring, truly caring, contributes to a successful life, because it gives life, whether academics, athletics, or social experiences, real meaning and purpose. Caring enough to take stock of who we are and what our children and surrounding adults really see in us may help during those moments of reflection, after our children become adults.

As educational leaders we need to realize that a life well lived comes from an early commitment to caring. It will involve risk, sacrifice, trust and a willingness to give others the benefit of the doubt. But it is key. As leaders, it is one more thing to think about in the evening when you attempt to go to sleep.

Sometimes life tosses you the unexpected. That is really when you learn the most about who you are. If you want to lead, and lead by example, you have to truly care.

Nicholas joined the Marines.

Nicholas went back to Indiana University.

Nicholas' unit was called to active duty a year later a couple days before Christmas.

Nicholas went to Iraq and came back.

He finished college and graduated from law school.

He just finished six years as a Marine Reservist as of the date of this publication.

He cares.

Create a Climate of Confidence.

Are you someone that educators can trust? Do you keep your promises and "walk the talk" in word and deed? Do your actions speak louder than your words? Do you have a formula for gaining the confidence of your colleagues? One such formula for building confidence in a school leader, which subsequently affects the school climate, might look like this:

Respect + Honesty + Credibility + Consistency = Confidence in the Leader

Building confidence in a school setting is a difficult, time-consuming, but essential task, whereas lack of confidence in the leader can infect you as quickly as the flu. Confidence is not automatic just because you are in a position of school leader, nor is it necessarily reciprocal (because I have confidence in you, you should have confidence in me). Additionally, even if you are visionary and have the charisma to lead, if the confidence between individuals with whom you work is lacking, your days as a school leader may be numbered. Confidence is built on a foundation of respect and trust for all individuals who work in the school setting, including parents, students, crossing guards, and cafeteria workers. As confidence in the leader is developed, the leader is seen as a person of influence. In other words, over time a school leader earns confidence because of the credibility that he or she has developed from being predicable, dependable, and honest, and then one can move to accomplishing tasks in the school through the confidence in the leader. Others become confident, too, and more professionally self-assured.

Recovering from a lack of confidence in the leader can be overwhelming, daunting, and, in some situations, impossible. For example, a school leader who consistently exaggerates at meetings about school successes, or who uses school property such as technological equipment for personal use, loses the opportunity to gain confidence from others and clearly fosters an environment of "no confidence" through unethical conduct. Over time these situations severely damage the human relationships at school and taint the ability of the leader to lead. Like a bad case of the flu, someone will catch the incident, spread "it" to others, and before you know it, everyone will be infected with "it." The misdeed or immoral action contaminates the school climate.

To be an effective school leader you need to develop a climate of confidence in the area in which you work and among all with whom you interact. Do you remember the Elvis Presley song, *Suspicious Minds?* One of the lines in the song says, "We can't go on together with suspicious minds." Are you singing it now? That lyric reminds us of the hard work of building a climate of confidence in schools and the outcome of what can happen if ignored.

Don't Undo Your Life's Work.

Administrators, teachers, and all those considered school leaders, like rabbis, priests, and other clergy, should be held to the highest moral and ethical standards. As role models, our colleagues and students look to us to be *the* example of doing what is right. The "Doing the Right Thing Buck" has to stop somewhere, and it should stop with you. Those in our service looking for sage advice will question all that we say and do if we have committed a moral blunder.

Moral improprieties, be they related to honesty, decency, or fidelity, cause followers to question and potentially ignore all that we say and do. In short, one cannot lead with a cloud of immorality over one's head. The news media contains stories of sexual liberties by teachers and administrators with their students, educators caught stealing school funds and storing it in their homes, and school personnel cheating on exams by changing student answers. These examples of poor moral decision making not only cause followers to not follow but also casts a shadow on the individual's past performance, even if it was stellar.

Because we are human, erring in typical daily decision making can occur with little risk to our leadership aura. In other words we have latitude to make mistakes as long as we did our best and have a history of well thought out, inclusive and moral decision making. People can make mistakes and life usually goes on. There is also a significant difference between a mistake and a difference of opinion. Frequently, those who disagree with us are doing so on matters of personal judgment—much of which is not even right or wrong but simply opinion like the teaching schedule that one does not like or the budget cuts that come down on us from on high. A moral lapse, on the other hand, is cause for extreme concern, because morality, like virginity, is absolute. Once lost, it cannot be regained. Your work in schools is to serve and be the best servant leader you can be. One moral impropriety can undo all your hard work. If you can't be viewed as a moral leader, you will not be viewed as a school leader.

Establish an Ethic of Compassion.

Being compassionate for people with whom you work and associate is a deep human relationship. Feelings of connection can foster close personal relationships in a school setting. When you are compassionate about someone in the school organization, department, classroom, or community, the message is clear: "I am interested in you and I am going to watch over you. I care that you are ill, unhappy, or frazzled, and how you feel is of concern to me."

One important role of the school leader is to foster an environment of compassion—compassion about students, compassion about custodians, compassion about families and adults in the school organization and community. Like the base coat when painting a wall, a caring environment is the basis for the social and emotional well being of the individuals with whom the school leader works. If no one cares, basic human needs are not being met. Who doesn't want someone to be interested in him or her! However, the act of compassion can take on a life of its own for a school leader; therefore, a word of caution is necessary.

Expressing compassion for others can be a full-time job; so much so that a school leader can become distracted from the job he or she was hired to do. Becoming too involved in each person's life can be exhausting, intrusive, and counterproductive. Effective school leaders find a balance between showing compassion for others, taking care of themselves and meeting the responsibilities of their work.

School leaders that have an ethic of compassion influence the social/emotional development of the individuals in their charge. The compassionate way in which individuals interact with each other conveys implicit messages about respect, trust and responsibility which seem to be able to surmount critical problems such as how to meet the *No Child Left Behind* categories with failing students or a potential suicide crisis. This ethic of compassion automatically clicks in for a school leader because it already exists waiting to be called upon. When individuals are beaten down and unable to think clearly, this principle of compassion can help give a school leader needed direction. Compassion counts. An ethic of deep compassion counts even more.

Exercise the Powers of a Superhero.

"Look up in the sky. It's a bird! It's a plane! It's Superman!"

More than five decades ago the television series *Superman* debuted. Many Americans grew up watching the "man of steel" fight crime with the assistance of his friends at the *Daily Planet*. As the TV show stated in the introductions—Superman stood for truth, justice, and the American way.

Moral and ethical school leaders may feel at times they need Superman or Superwoman abilities on a daily basis to do a good job of leading. Too bad school leaders can't muster up and reap the benefits from the numerous superhero powers Superman possessed. Standing for truth, justice, and the American way may sound noble, but isn't that what we should all stand for. Although no one will call you Superman or Superwoman in your daily struggles to be a moral and ethical leader, if you stand for truth, justice, and the American way, people should call you just that (at least it would sound cool even though it will never happen). And of these three qualities, truth is the one that is most important and the one that will help you the most on your leadership journey.

You should not need Superman's X-ray vision to see the truth. The truth is something that should be easily discernible. You should not need Superman's superhearing powers to be able to hear the truth coming from your lips. It should flow naturally. You should not worry that kryptonite (that rock stuff from Superman's home planet which rendered him powerless) will appear to you in the form of your daily stresses and ruin your reputation or adversely impact your job security. It is not worth worrying about. You should not need to leap buildings in a single bound. Sometimes at the end of the day we are lucky to just be able to walk out the door. You should not need Superman's strength but settle for the strength that truth brings. You should not need bullets to bounce off your chest but rather criticisms to bounce off your feelings as if you were made of metal. And while we could all use Superman's ability to fly because we have to be in so many places at once, just settle for being honest in one place at a time. In the end, tell the truth and you will be recognized as having superpower ability to lead and you will be known as an honest person. In today's day and age with so much deceit and immoral conduct, telling the truth—just being plain honest at all times—is a simple skill, albeit involved in complex processes, that will clearly and absolutely help you become a great leader.

Great school leaders need to tell the truth. And similar to the old TV show *To Tell the Truth* where three people would all pretend to be have the same identity and the panel would ask questions to see who was the real person (for us older people the show would end with, "And would the real *[insert person's name here]* please stand up." The truth is that the truth of a matter is what counts and you should be counted on to tell the truth. Just be truthful, at all times, in all places, and in all circumstances. You will be pleasantly surprised what happens to your reputation and ability to lead.

Experience Empathy.

The ability to know how another person honestly feels is a most valuable interpersonal skill for a school leader. Television commercials convince you to feel as happy as the person using a special deodorant or as sad as the caveman who is being mistreated in a restaurant to the nightly news of victims of gang violence. We are bombarded daily with opportunities to feel and experience various messages from and about people. This constant media bombardment can make us numb to the realities, challenges and pains of those who surround us.

Sorting and paying attention to these messages can help us in making judgments and taking proper action in a school setting. One instance that comes to mind is when a school leader has to deliver "bad news" that an employee may be losing his or her job. An empathetic school leader should be attuned and prepared for the impact of what he or she is going to say, how he or she is going to say it, and how the message will be received. For example, the leader could sympathetically say, "I am sorry things have worked out this way. I do care and feel bad about the situation." Yes, you can deliver "bad news" without being hurtful and destructive and at the same time follow the legal guidelines. The goal should be to reduce defensiveness, bitterness, and resentment by asking simple questions of yourself like, "How would I like to be treated in this situation?" "How would I feel if I were in his or her shoes?" You should consider rehearsing the exact words you plan to say and pretend you are hearing the words being delivered to you by another. Watch your body language and voice intonation, as the majority of the message and the additional inferences of the message will come from the delivery. On which side of the desk are you sitting? Messages delivered from the same side of the desk give the appearance of being more personal and caring. Of course, not every school leader will have the same sureness and expertise in these skills. But seeing things from another person's perspective and actually hearing the feelings of what is being said is a significant and powerful skill for school leaders.

Gain Acceptance by Making Moral and Ethical Decisions.

The day comes and the day goes and with it decisions that affect the lives of many. Classroom teachers and building administrators alike make countless decisions that have near and far reaching implications for those in their stead. We all know what it is like to be on the "short end of the stick." A decision that filters its way down to us that appears to defy common sense, does not ring true to our beliefs, appears politically motivated, is not in the best interest of children and, on occasion, may even seem personal. After taking a deep breath our first reaction may be to argue the decision. Another reaction may be to just criticize the decision maker(s). Another way to deal with the rejection may be to just complain to those with whom we work or socialize. In any event we are not happy, may feel cheated, and frequently will have negative feelings for the person or persons associated with making the decision. So what can help the person responsible for the decision to move that decision from unacceptable to either marginally acceptable or even a state of neutrality? What helps in situations like this is to ensure that the decision is fundamentally grounded in an ethical and moral principle.

For example, a decision made and stated in terms of being "fair" for all involved can be easier to accept. A decision that is shared by saying I have to be "honest" with myself first may be easier to accept. A decision that may have been made for financial reasons may be couched in terms that the integrity of the fiscal system cannot be compromised, or, in other words, we just don't have the money. Some decisions require the wisdom of Solomon and could be shared based upon the ethic of "I am just doing the best I can." If the decision is based on what is best for children, and it is truly in their best interest, then your moral resolve will be demonstrated. If you can say I did it because it was the right thing to do, it was the only choice in good consciousness, it was a decent decision and any other decision would have been unacceptable to me as a person of virtuous stance, you will go a long way to at least getting to neutral ground on the recipient's part. *Less upset, a state of neutrality,* and *marginally acceptable* are still better outcomes than *more upset* and *not acceptable at all*. Your decisions can be accepted and viewed as fair under these circumstances. Sometimes the best one can do is just move on, call it a day and say, "I did the best I could."

Have a Steadfast System of Beliefs.

For nearly three decades I have begun each morning with a drive northbound on Sunset Ridge Road. I worry about the traffic, our children's safety, and pray that no child will be injured during the course of the day. I worry that school will be a good place academically, socially, and emotionally for our children, and that all the decisions will be the right ones. I worry that my colleagues will be in peace, be in good health, and have a good day. This daily routine is reminiscent of the movie *Groundhog Day* starring Bill Murray. Everything is the same—everything, that is, until I get to school. The boring commute is always transformed into problem solving a unique set of circumstances that make *Groundhog Day* long forgotten. While there may be similarities between and among circumstances, each human being is unique and each set of problems is different. To think otherwise reduces our complex profession to a set of conditions that will never pay justice to the work we do.

In our profession one never knows what's around the corner. So what can you do to help you get through each day? The one thing that you can bring to each day, each set of circumstances, and each problem is your steadfast belief system. You better know who you are and what you stand for. Although every day will be challenging—one day you may wake up and take that same boring trip to work only to find yourself later that evening on every news channel attempting to articulate the unique events of the day—events that you were not responsible for creating but responsible for resolving. You will then read about it in the newspaper the next day. You may even by on the front page. You will ask yourself how did this happen to me. You will question what lies ahead and you will certainly long for *Groundhog Day*.

So how do you get through that day or several days as it may be? How do you withstand the constant pressure, turmoil and uncertainty that will clearly tear at the very core of your person? How do you go without sleep? How do live knowing that you are just doing your job and you are a good person. Well, it's simple. Know thyself and make sure you are a person of impeccable character, morals, ethics, and values. Because sometimes at the end of the day (even if the day does not end but just leads to the next), you will know who you are, what you stand for, believe, and realize—that is all you need. And guess what—you will get though it.

Lead with Your Moral Compass.

My mother always told me "If you have a mouth, you are never lost." I have put those words of wisdom into practice on many occasions. I think she should have also added a lesson on how to read people via their body language. Someone once told me that 82% of a person's message comes form their voice intonation and physical appearance while delivering the message. I could usually tell quickly when asking for directions whether or not the person knew what they were talking about or were just hoping to be helpful. For example, did the person speak the directions quickly to me with deliberation and conviction? Did the person possess some personal knowledge of the place I was going to? Did they mention things I would pass along the way? Did the person speak with assurance and conviction? In any event, I have suggested to my own children that they can use their grandmother's plan as a back up but it's best to just get a map (or better yet a GPS [global positioning system]!). But what ever happened to that good old-fashioned compass? How does it know to point north? It has something to do with the fact that the compass needle is a magnet and it points to the North Pole because the earth core is filled with dense iron and gives off a magnetic field. That was simple right—not!

The core of an educational leader should have magnetic moral and ethical magna that allows the brain to immediately sense the moral and ethicalness of an issue and, thus, rapidly direct the brain to formulate the correct commentary. It should be automatic—no wavering here. A moral compass always points north; it knows right from wrong and how to quickly weave through the shades of gray. It provides the educational leader with a charismatic quality that people will be attracted to because the followers will know that a sense of correctness and trust will always be there. The people with whom you are surrounded will never feel lost or see you at a loss for words. They will not be checking your body language and sizing up you and your commentary. They will simply say, there goes an honest person—an always-honest person. I trust that person and the direction I am being led.

Listen to Your Mother.

Can't you just hear your mother saying, "If you can't say something nice—just don't say anything at all." Those words always seem to echo at a time when you really question whether saying something not so nice would feel so much better. As educational leaders it behooves us to be role models to all those who surround us by just being plain nice. We are all on this earth for a short period of time and as we search for meaning, for a reason to understand why we were put here, doesn't it just make sense to be courteous, respectful, kind, and polite to all those we meet along the way. Doesn't it make sense to try to brighten the days of others by just being upbeat and positive? And not just by the words you choose, but how you say them as well. Voice intonation and body language usually tell us a lot more about what you are thinking than what you actually say. It is most important to feel the words as well as say the words. Pleasant bedside manners certainly make a visit to a doctor a more enjoyable experience. Friendly service certainly makes a trip to a restaurant a happier occasion. A smile certainly goes a long way at a parent teacher conference even when delivering unpleasant news. A pleasing hello from a receptionist at the dentist's office certainly starts that visit off right even if you are leaving there numb.

Consequently, it does not take any more energy to be nice than to be otherwise. A smile on your face lets the other person know that there is a warm, friendly, caring person on the other side waiting to be of assistance. In our profession, one would think that being nice is certainly a critical state of being worth having and demonstrating on a daily basis. As an educational leader we want to reach out and be that friendly conscientious person who wants to be known as a positive sole. It is reminiscent of the driver who lets you in a traffic lane when traffic is congested. Or the person who lets you in the checkout line when you only have one item to buy and your spouse or significant other is just waiting for it at home. Or even the person who just opens a door for you when you are in a hurry and says, "Please, you first." Education should be *the* profession where courtesy, respect, kindness, and politeness are "paid forward" every day. If we can't do this because it is in our heart and soul, we should at least do it because it is right for us to do so. Honor your mother by demonstrating that you were listening when she gave you advice.

Protect Your Bonds of Trust.

In God We Trust—the bold phrase that our nation "coined" during the civil war for our currency reflects on the importance of trust. Trust is the key word that the *Merriam-Webster's Collegiate Dictionary* (11th ed., p. 1344) defines as a "assured reliance on the character, ability, strength, or truth of someone or something." A best friend asks you, "Can you keep a secret?" She trusts that you will listen and respond accordingly, perhaps with compassion, perhaps with a suggestion, but, most importantly, with her best interests in mind and the knowledge that it will go no further. A teacher you work with confides in you that there is a challenging event in her life—a divorce, a life-threatening illness, a recurring problem with a parent or principal that she needs someone to talk with in confidence. Coming to you should be therapeutic, encouraging, sympathetic, and rewarding. Most importantly, however, the old adage that this is "between you and me" must be honored. The key element in any of these conversations that makes this "work" is trust. Without the bond of trust that exists between two people that gives them the intimacy of knowing that the entire conversation will remain confident from the get-go and be from the heart, soul, and mind, it just does not work. What causes that bond of trust to exist is your moral and ethical fiber, that foundation within you that must be firm, grounded and unflappable.

If you want to lead, you have to have a following. In our profession people will follow you if they "have to" but, in that case, the lounge conversation will frequently turn to finding ways around the leader and around the system. We are referring here to a leader who is leader in title or position only. True leadership, inspirational leadership, comes from an individual who people know has a strong moral and ethical fiber and, as such, can be trusted. You don't want to be known as that used car salesman or that "flim-flam" carnival operator that no one trusts. The next time a child comes to you with a concern think about why that student chose you. The next time a friend asks for your advice, think about why it was you that the friend chose to be the person to talk with. While pondering these situations, ponder the outcomes. You will either be trusted or not; it's that simple. It takes a lot to gain a person's trust and little to lose it. Protect your bonds of trust as if they were your reputation, because they are, and, along with it, your ability to lead.

Respect Everyone.

It's difficult to think about respect without remembering the classic song from Aretha Franklin, the Queen of Soul, titled *R-E-S-P-E-C-T*. In that song she asks the listener to "find out what it means to me" as she keeps singing and chanting about the importance of respect. As the beat of the song continues, she sings and asks for "just a little bit" of respect from someone who has ignored her and made her feel rejected.

Unfortunately, all of us probably have memories of being made to feel small and unimportant. One doesn't have to go far to see turmoil on the playground, cyberbullying, harassment among students in the hallways, gestures and inappropriate language toward teachers and students, teachers gossiping about a particular individual, someone who has a physical abnormality, disregard for school rules and those who must enforce them, individuals from other ethnicities—who look different, have an accent, possibly dress differently from the mainstream and are "made fun of." Certainly there are other school examples of disrespect that could be listed, but the reality is these events are a small part of the mirror reflecting our lack of civility as a society.

The school and more specifically the environment in which everyone comes to each day needs to be respected. It is the responsibility of the moral and ethical school leader to see that this happens. This means honoring every individual who comes to the school door, happy that he or she has arrived, and appreciating the individual's values and differences that are brought to the organization. After all, people are the school and without them, the school is just vacant space made of bricks and mortar. Students should observe the adults in the school as role models who show respect toward each other. They should witness adults behaving in ways that the school culture deems polite and courteous. In turn, these respectful relationships will breed more respect until, at last, respect is woven into the fabric of the everyday way of life of the school.

Is this utopia? Not at all. Think about what respect means to you. Show respect—and *not just a little bit*—toward teachers, parents (even the problem parents), superintendents, school board members, principals, administrators, crossing guards, bus drivers, cafeteria workers, volunteers, coaches, custodians, school nurses and secretaries, assistants, delivery persons, security guards, and, of course, students. Respect everyone for all they bring and all they do each day for the good and well being of the school.

Seek and Discover the Truth from Complaints.

"My child is so bored in your room. Why can't you challenge him? He's gifted you know. And I don't just mean gifted; I mean profoundly gifted. His pediatrician told me so."

"There is too much homework in Mrs. Smith's class. Don't you agree?"

"Why didn't my son get a valentine from all the students in his room? He's being bullied by several students in class."

"Your dances are too loud and my child is surely losing some of his hearing."

"Why do you start school so early?"

"Why do you start school so late?"

"Why can't the busses be on time?"

"Why are your cafeteria lines so long? And by the way, don't you care about nutrition—why aren't there more meatballs in the spaghetti? My daughter never has enough time to eat her lunch."

Tired of those nagging complaints. Wouldn't you just like to say, "You can take this complaint and _____ _____." or "Don't you have something better to do with your life." Well, it's time for the *complaint paradigm shift*.

For starters think about the last time you made a complaint. Think about whom you went to, why you were there, and ultimately what (if anything) was resolved. How did you feel? Frustrated? Aggravated (or as my father-in-law used to say, "I'm really *irrigated!*")? You obviously felt justified in your complaint, but did you feel that the complaint resolver was empathetic? How would you have felt if the person said, "I understand how you feel and let's get to the bottom of what happened"? Try this on for size: "I don't understand what you went through but I am here to help and I really do care."

When faced with a complaint, you have a choice. You can build a bridge or create a river of troubled waters. A moral and ethical leader will take the time to ferret out the complaint because it will build a relationship with the person, which, ultimately, may pay big dividends for a child—and that's why we are all here. And guess what, somewhere in that complaint usually lies a shred of truth. A morsel of integrity that will make your school a better place. Think about these answers to the above scenarios:

A child may or may not be gifted, but is bored.

A child is spending too much time doing homework, but not because too much is being given.

The child is saddened because he didn't get one valentine and everybody laughed at him.

A child's mother feels the dances are too loud and, guess what, an audiometer revealed that, at times, the music was in the danger zone.

One tired child is affected by an early start time, while another child is an early riser. Both are both equally affected by start times.

A child has been waiting, along with others, way too long in a lunch line and there is a simple solution but no one took the time to care or think of it.

A child's mother is a nutritionist and there should be more protein in the lunch.

A moral and ethical leader takes the time to look into *all* complaints. Not just the ones that seem right on the surface but also the ones that seem off the wall and downright ridiculous. Yes, it might take time—a lot of time—to investigate, but time is life's currency and this is a good use of it. And by the way, complainers are not always looking for immediate responses; they are frequently looking for empathizers. They are looking for someone who cares; someone who will take the time to investigate the alleged concern; someone who will get back and say, "I care, I have looked into the situation and here's what I found." And, guess what, everybody wins. You build a relationship that benefits the child and in many, many instances makes things a little bit better for everyone else. Before you know it, you are known as someone who cares deeply about children and the entire school system. Someone who wants to make a difference and is respected by everyone. You have become that "go to" moral and ethical leader who makes a difference and improves the system one small discovery at a time. It is usually not the big things in life that are the problems; it's usually the little things.

Stand Up for Integrity.

Warren Buffett once said that the three important qualities in a manager are integrity, intelligence, and energy. But without the first, he cautioned, the other two will kill you (Bolman & Deal, 2002, p. 23).

Without integrity, you might as well begin writing your eulogy so that people have the written word in front of them to remember you by rather than their keen observations and conclusions. "Here lies Mary Jones. She was a good school leader until...."

Integrity is the main ingredient for a school leader who is looking for a recipe for professional leadership success. It is a life staple having been cultivated at birth, advanced with age, and seasoned in the halls of school. Like an umbrella it protects other character values such as honesty, truthfulness, trustworthiness, and honor, and is your constant companion.

Integrity isn't optional in school leadership. One might expect, or even excuse, a recent college graduate who slightly exaggerates work experience on his or her resume or a new teacher who chooses to be liked more than respected in order to help students, but the person who is leading a school, department, team, or classroom and whose leadership may have a lifelong effect on every child, parent, and taxpayer is held to a higher standard.

Just for starters, the school community wants a school leader to be smart, unbiased, accessible, penny pinching, sensitive, articulate, well groomed, and child-centered. But at the most basic level, school leaders must have integrity. You don't get to take a pass on your integrity. Not on certain days, not ever. You can't be a little bit honest, but honest everyday, demonstrating integrity in the decisions made for the welfare and best interests of children. Even universities are asking their professors and instructors to teach ethics lessons and to take ethics tests annually.

Leaders with integrity exemplify the messages they preach—they walk the talk, lead by example, and expect others to do the same. They use power in ethical ways as stewards of the school in which they work and demonstrate that they are held responsible for results whether others are successful or not. For example, a school leader with integrity would not hold an excellent teacher's job over his or her head just because testing results of a class did not meet state standards on a state exam. A school leader with integrity would handle government grants with care and abide by its rules and reports. Colleagues, school employees, parents, or students would not be the brunt of jokes or unflattering humor in the faculty lounge.

In today's education world, the public wants to see your integrity—your code of ethics worn proudly each day like a brag vest. Giving lip service to integrity is like walking out of a store without paying. Not getting caught stealing from a store may work once in a while, but eventually you will get caught. Stealing from your integrity puts you in compromising situations and jeopardizes your life's work.

Stay the Moral Ground.

Abraham Lincoln always made decisions that he thought were in the best interest of our country. "Honest Abe" never strayed from his patriotic duty and consistently stood on the right side of an issue. Fortunately, we have to make numerous decisions on a daily basis that are significantly less complicated, certainly not life-threatening, and usually with less than earth-shattering implications and no fanfare. You know those small-talk things—water cooler commentary that comes and goes. Those items that just pop up in the teachers' lounge or quickly pass you by when a teacher, secretary, custodian, or cook are making small talk about something in the hallway. The problem is that it is frequently easier to just agree with a colleague, parent, or supervisor than it is to disagree. Sometimes it is also much easier to just not say anything at all. It also may be more mainstream to be polite and just smile or nod and say "sure, whatever." So what if the person thinks you agree with him? Maybe you do, maybe you don't. You didn't commit yourself one way or the other—or so you think. It is just easier to save yourself and what little energy you have left in a day for the big things—the ones that really matter. You know the ones worth fighting for. The ones you would be upset with yourself for not standing up for the next morning when you wake up. The ones your mother would really be upset with you if you did not stand up for. Well, there is a problem here Houston. The problem is that your actions and inactions as well are all important. They all have meaning in becoming the consciousness of your moral persona as viewed by others. They become you, and you they. In short you are required to speak up and answer in many situations.

If a person steals something, whether it is a large sum of money or a penny, that person is still a thief. If a person lies, whether it is a big lie or a white lie, that person is still a liar. If a person cheats, whether it is copying one answer or an entire paper, that person is still a cheater. If a person makes advances on another person, whether it is just flirting or a serious attempt, that person is still being aggressive. It is best in our profession to simply stay on moral ground and not provide anyone with even a hint of immoral behavior. Our standards must be of the highest caliber. Our role as a leader, a hero for some, should not be tainted by even the smallest hint of impropriety. You are either moral or you are not.

Take the Honesty Test.

Honesty is the best policy when it comes to being a school leader and making everyday decisions. There really is no better policy. In actuality school leaders are put on an "honor system" every day that they walk through the door of a school because of the trust that has been given to them in the position defined as *school leader*. Parents trust school leaders to make honest decisions that take care of the social, emotional, and academic needs of their children. Teachers trust that school leaders will make honest decisions in which they will be treated fairly and equitably as a faculty member. Students trust that school leaders are making honest decisions that will benefit them educationally now and in the future. Being dishonest means that an individual has compromised his or her moral and ethical code and now sits in a position of mistrust and disfavor. As quickly as stakeholders in a school can trust you, it can go away. Why would educators want to put themselves in such a compromising position?

In a typical school day school leaders on the honor system make hundreds of decisions and many earn disfavor, doubt and suspicion instead of accolades, confidence, conviction and faith. How will you fare? The *Honesty Test* below will give you a sense of where you might stand in your moral and ethical framework as an honest person. Are you up for the challenge? Are these statements true or false about you? Let's be honest here!

HONESTY TEST

T F 1. I state things that are true; I don't misrepresent facts to benefit myself or others. (Example: I don't say that our school/department/grade level is doing fine on state tests when in fact some groups of children are struggling.)

T F 2. I apply fair and equitable treatment to everyone, including students, parents, and teachers. (Example: If a parent requests that a child leave school early for the day, I am consistent and fair in honoring similar requests.)

T F 3. I act in a truthful manner, not in ways that could be perceived as misleading others. (Example: I canceled a faculty meeting stating that it is unnecessary; however, in reality I have a personal appointment.)

T F 4. I don't blame others as scapegoats for my weaknesses. (Example: I don't blame the committee when curriculum work is not complete because of my setting unrealistic timelines for the committee.)

T F 5. I don't live on "good intentions." (Example: "I intended to tell you about the report, but I got busy.")

T F 6. I don't tell "white lies/half-truths." (Example: I don't say there is not enough money in the budget when actually I just don't want to give the person the money.)

T F 7. I don't pressure faculty, staff, students, or parents in situations that might make them defensive or prone to lie. (Example: I don't say to a teacher that his or her test scores are not as high as those of the other teachers on my team.)

T F 8. I don't enter into a debate with myself trying to rationalize why lying is a better alternative to telling the truth. (Example: No one will really notice if I was late to work.)

T F 9. I don't falsify records, test scores, report cards, parent–teacher conference reports, or other school documents.

T F 10. I do what I say will do. (Example: I follow through.)

If you answered "true" to all ten questions, you have passed the Honesty Test with flying colors. If you were close to passing the Honesty Test, you need to review and consider the failing statement as an area for personal and professional improvement. Honesty is the key factor in building a trusting and long-lasting relationship required to lead and succeed.

Tell the Truth, the Whole Truth, and Nothing but the Truth.

Oyez! Oyez! Court is now in session. Please place your left hand on the *Bible*, raise your right hand, and say: I solemnly swear to tell the truth, the whole truth, and nothing but the truth so help me God.

Each day as you walk through the doors of your school pretend you are in a court of law and the bailiff is swearing you in. Just keep in mind that you are obligated to tell the truth, the whole truth, and nothing but the truth either because it's ethically and morally the right thing to do or because you are under the penalty of perjury if you do not. Think to yourself—the entire truth does matter—not just the easy pieces that make a conversation comfortable and risk free but also all the pieces that complete the entire truth puzzle.

Don't we always try to discover the truth in disciplinary matters with children? Don't you just hate it when Johnny says Jack did it? Jack says Johnny did it. And the truth be known that after a lengthy interrogation they were both involved and so were a host of others and it all began on the way to school or on the Internet with an email or online chat, which can be so impersonal and with little worry about hurting another's feelings. And the truth came to light when you got serious with them and used the technique of putting the two of them in chairs and had the children face each other and talk it out. (*Tip:* You may need more time if girls are involved [past histories are rarely forgotten].) Getting to the bottom of the truth is really important to a fair, just, and complete resolution of a matter. Haven't you ever said, "Just tell me the truth and we can work this out." Well, practice what you preach. Discretion is *not* the better part of valor here.

As leaders we must be forthright in our conversations with our colleagues—even when that creates a problem. Don't you trust more the person who is candid than the one who plays candid camera—the one who does not reveal the entire truth? Isn't it more important to take the "hit" when you tell someone that the lesson did need improvement; or that classroom management was lacking; or that you really do not appreciate what was said; or that you disagree with this or that; or you need some space here; or no, it wasn't perfect; or that you don't think that matches; or just suck it up—life can be tough!

Tell the truth, the whole truth, and nothing but the truth and you will be trusted. With that trust you will be empowered to lead, and with that leading, you will be in a position to make a difference. And you will never be the brunt of that old joke, "You can tell when an administrator is lying—his lips move!"

Value and Demonstrate Appreciation for Others.

A moral and ethical leader, by virtue of his or her own honorable life and leadership abilities, has legitimate authority that goes well beyond any school board's ability to offer financial remuneration to its employees. How can that be?

I have always contended that money is not a satisfier—only a dissatisfier. If one is not compensated at a level that one believes is adequate and fair (as determined by a comparison of like position and with other like school districts), then one will be dissatisfied and, subsequently, unhappy. School comparisons are important but they can only take us so far. How can you complete the journey or, in some cases, compensate for lack of compensation? The following two examples will shed some light on this question and the essence of human nature.

Renee Montero feels great about being the school's custodian. He is happy, alert, and always goes the extra mile for "his" students, teachers, and school. Why? Well he is a wonderful human being by nature but the icing on the cake is that the teachers and children, modeled by their principal, demonstrate a daily dose of servant leadership. Renee is always made to feel important. Why, because he is; it is that simple. We are all human beings just trying to do the best job we can everyday. Renee laughs and jokes with the principal; sometimes they even take turns bowing to each other. The children understand (not just know) that Renee is an important fellow human being and a critical part of "our" school and that his service has value and merit. They say please, thank you, and how are you to him everyday. For the most part they pick up after themselves and realize that character comes in many forms and it all starts with the dignity and respect we have for each other.

Mary Brown is the school's cook. She works hard to ensure that the right food is prepared at the right time and in the right manner. Mary cares. Mary cares so much that she even knows what each child likes to eat. For decades the school principal began each day with all classes taking the daily lunch count. Students are asked who is buying their lunch (what items are they buying) and if they want milk. One day the principal was in the kitchen and asked Mary how the lunch count was coming that day. She politely told him that she never pays any attention to it. Although there is a menu change every day, she knew each child (give or take a bit) and what each child would eat. Why take lunch count? Years of wasted time taking lunch counts under the heading "we've always done it that way." In return for her keen interest and genuine concern for "her" children, the students have great respect for Mary and treat her with the utmost courtesy. They say please and thank you in the lunch lines and sing *Happy Birthday* loudly on that special day. This mutual feeling is symbiotic and makes for a wonderful school lunch period and sets the tone for the afternoon for that matter.

Mutual respect and demonstrating value for others starts with a moral and ethical school leader. It is contagious, has value and merit, and is the difference that goes well beyond what the dollar has to offer. And better yet, it costs nothing.

3

On Dealing with Stress

Just walk down the halls, visit classrooms, or chat with school administrators of any school on any given day in any given year and you can feel "it" in the corridors and classrooms, sense "it" in the voice intonations, and see "it" on the expressions of so many faces. "It" may come from the child worried about safety, an exam, an upcoming dance or competition, a newfound blemish, or the clothing choice that day. "It" may be the teacher leader concerned for a child, a lesson gone awry, a personal problem, a health issue, or a financial challenge. "It" may be a school administrator struggling with a personnel problem, a student that is on the verge of suspension, a tripped fire alarm, a *No Child Left Behind* report, an upcoming budget meeting or just trying to juggle a harried schedule. "It" is stress. "It" is pervasive and that easy-to-feel sensation that lurks in school buildings because of so much to do, so little time and the multitude and complexity of large numbers of students and adults each exponentially adding to the stress factor continuum with their own concerns and problems. And the school leader tends to be the person who takes it all in and tries to be the problem solver and that compassionate caring person for others.

Let's take just take a look at one example of imposed stress. The *No Child Left Behind Act* puts pressure on the entire educational establishment, and specifically on school leaders, by requiring them to demonstrate academic progress toward state competency exams for all students in grades three through twelve. By the year 2014 this standards-based education reform from the federal government requires all tested students to reach 100% "adequate yearly progress" in reading and math. Albeit a noble goal, would anyone want to put money on that happening? This is but one of the multitude of stressors that school leaders must address in addition to their day-to-day leadership of trying to keep the school doors open.

Dan Lortie (2009), in Chapter 6 of his book *School Principal: Managing in Public*, discusses the difficulties of a school principal's job. He highlights numerous factors that reveal why the school principalship is so "hard." These include complicating conditions, the scarcity of time, interruptions, maintenance of order and safety, paperwork, complex tasks, mistakes, less-popular tasks, trouble (serious repercussions), and parents and teachers. Lortie discusses in great detail the problems associated with each of these variables. These variables, which Lortie categorizes as "Complications and Complexities," add to the daily and never-ending stress level of school leaders. Simply put, as Lortie so aptly states in his opening paragraph, "What is hard about being an elementary principal?" Obviously there is a lot!

According to the American Psychological Association Practice Organization (APAPO, 2007, p.1), "Stress is a fact of life, say 79 percent of those surveyed, and 73 percent believe that too much stress can make you sick. During the month preceding the survey, 77 percent of Americans experienced stress-related physical symptoms including fatigue, headache, and upset stomach. And 73 percent reported psychological symptoms including irritability or anger, feeling nervous and lack of energy" (http://www.apapractice.org/apo/in_the_news/apa_survey_fines_rising.html#).

How should a school leader manage the entourage of daily stress? As a school leader I questioned year after year how I transformed from a healthy person to one contracting bronchitis four to six times per year. I questioned the ritual of driving to the doctor's office only to witness the same routine with the same outcome. The prescription was always the same—250 milligrams of erythromycin four times a day for ten days. With the advent of Z-Packs, the remedy and recuperation period was so much better. Take two pills the first day and one each day for the next four. I never had to miss work. But why was I getting so sick, so often? Sure I was very busy, but was I under that much stress?

According to the 1978 President's Commission on Mental Health, "There is ample evidence that emotional stress is often related to physical illness and that many physical disorders coexist with psychological disorders." One needs only to search the Internet for the multitude of resources available to learn more about stress and how it affects you physically and mentally. According to the Mayo Clinic website, "If your mind and body are constantly on edge because of excessive stress in your life, you may face serious health problems. That's because your body's 'flight-or-fight reaction'— its natural alarm system— is constantly on." The site continues to state, "But when the stressors of your life are always present, leaving you constantly feeling stressed, tense, nervous, or on edge, that flight-or-fight reaction stays turned on. The less control you have over potentially stress-inducing events and the more uncertainty they create, the more likely you are to feel stressed. Even the typical day-to-day demands of living can contribute to your body's stress response." The site lists a number of health-related risks induced by stress, including heart disease, digestive problems, obesity, skin conditions, and memory impairment (http://www.mayoclinic.com/health/stress/sroooo1).

Robert Sapolsky (2004, p. 384), in *Why Zebras Don't Get Ulcers*, sums it up nicely when he states, "Stress can wreck havoc with your metabolism, raise your blood pressure, burst your white blood cells, make you flatulent, ruin your sex life, and if that's not enough possibly damage your brain. Why don't we throw in the towel right now?" I would contend the reason most of us don't throw in the towel is that we care deeply about our jobs, our contribution to humanity, and the expectations of our work.

In addition to the physical problems associated with stress for school leaders, because of their particular role in schools, the problem can become contagious and place the entire system under stress. According to Kelehear (2004, p. 32), "When leaders are in a high state of stress, they create a culture that is under stress as well. Schools that regularly function in an atmosphere of unmanaged stress begin to be dysfunctional and unhealthy. Teachers' attitudes and morale deteriorate. Administrators and teachers cease communicating. Students feel ignored and unsafe. The whole school becomes 'tired,' filled with frustrated and angry teachers and students." The author continues to state that, "What becomes clear when coming to terms with stress and its related consequences is that stress can destroy morale and enthusiasm in a school. Unmanaged stress debilitates teachers and students and dismantles their learning communities."

School leaders need to address their own stress and pay attention to signs and signals of stress around them. Unmanaged administrator stress can create a toxic school culture where communication between teachers and administrators diminishes, parking lot conversations appear, issues are not discussed but assumed, and gossip and speculation run rampant. Ironically, students begin to replicate how they feel and act out what they see. I can remember as a novice teacher asking the school secretary each morning if it was a good day or bad day to see the principal, meaning was the principal in a good or bad mood that day. Thumbs up from the secretary meant that the principal was in a good mood; thumbs down meant enter at your own risk.

Controlling stress means understanding that the school environment is in a constant state of pressure, which imposes serious consequences on you physically, psychologically, emotionally, and socially. It impairs your ability to lead effectively, by robbing you of your precious energy and neglecting your personal needs. So often you cannot change the external conditions of a school day such as a meeting that goes off-track, a parent who threatens to sue you, or another report due with a short deadline. But you can control your internal reaction to the pressure.

This chapter contains many suggestions for addressing the physical, psychological, emotional, and social needs that interfere with maintaining balance and gaining control over your everyday school stress. There are some usual suggestions offered from time management to eating healthy and exercising regularly, which are not exclusive to school leaders but need to be mentioned. There are other bits of advice, which call upon abilities to stay calm and deal effectively with the relationships you have with people. Finally, there are suggestions offered to mentally challenge you to think differently about your stressful school situation. Your view, outlook, attitude, and demeanor are critical to your ability to withstand stressors. Again, this chapter challenges you to reflect on your stress and enter it into your personal framework for leading. Remember that a dead school leader serves no one.

Act Calm, Cool, and Collected.

Most of us have heard of the story of Chicken Little who was hit on the head with an acorn and thought the sky was falling. As she began to spread the word about the sky, she created alarm and panic with her barnyard friends and throughout the countryside.

This type of behavior is very common in the landscape of schools. In fact, I think Chicken Little was probably in middle school. So many students in that preadolescent age group can be described as alarmists, drama kings and queens, or crisis junkies—those students who make a mountain out of molehill or leap automatically to conclusions that are negative, such as "I don't like the way she is looking at me; she must hate me."

Chicken Little needlessly worried about the looming danger of the falling sky and could do little but run around screaming and losing her cool. There are so many daily school situations in which it is easy to lose your cool. Consider, for example, Dr. Clyde, a superintendent of schools who is confident about his abilities to handle school board meetings, but at one meeting in particular the school board members stray from the agenda and begin to talk about a past topic of financing field trips. As Dr. Clyde reminds the board members of the agenda, four board members continue talking. Sitting in the audience, I can see that Dr. Clyde is beginning to show signs of agitation. A large vein on his forehead is beginning to pop out and his face is turning a bit red, but his voice demeanor is steady and calm. "I believe we need to move on," Dr. Clyde states. The board members continue to talk. Time goes by. Had it not been for a vein, I would not have known that Dr. Clyde was entering a panic mode and his blood pressure was rising. Everyone in the audience had their eyes fixed on Dr. Clyde. What was going to happen next? Is he losing control of the meeting? After a few minutes, the board members stopped their side conversations and got back to the tasks on the agenda, all the while Dr. Clyde remained patient, composed, and in control of himself. The situation passed calmly, as did the vein.

Parents, students, teachers, and the community will look to the school leader as the individual with the answer—the one to bring clarity, direction, and focus to a situation—and will not expect the leader to run around adding to the calamity. Many, many times, in one form or another, the sky will be falling in someone's life and you need to ask yourself this important question: "What convincing evidence do I have that this is true?" This statement does not mean that you have to hire a team of detectives to provide you with facts. After all Chicken Little did not say, "I think the sky is falling and I better call an astronomer to check!" Nor does it mean that a serious situation like the fire alarm going off or a child reported missing should be dismissed as frivolous. To continue in Chicken Little terms, you may not be able to prevent the acorns from falling on everyone's head, but you can control your actions and your reactions to the lumps by your calm, cool and collected demeanor.

Agree Politely to Disagree and Be a Broken Record.

At some point in our educational careers, we are all faced with challenging people. Take parents as an example. There are numerous times in our lives that we have to say "no." Maybe you are telling a parent that the child is not allowed to be in school because of an infectious disease. Maybe you are telling a parent that the child did not make an athletic team or get the part in a play. Maybe you are telling a parent their child didn't get that report card grade promised and it is not going to be changed. Maybe you are telling a parent that you won't change his or her classroom placement. The maybes are endless in our world.

Areas of disagreement can arise frequently during the normal course of our working day at all levels. Sometimes in the end the answer is simply "no." Simple, yeah right? No matter how much time you take, no matter how much you care, no matter how much you listen, sometimes, in the end, it really is that simple. However, the problem arises when the recipient just can't take "no" for an answer. Even when repeated, some people persist with trying to change your mind. You are thinking to yourself what part of the word "no" doesn't this person understand. You might even feel like quoting Chris Rock from the movie *Rush Hour* and dramatically say, "Do you understand the words that are coming out of my mouth?"

In situations like this, you do not want ambiguity to be part of the equation. For example, your job may require you to dismiss an employee. It's challenging to do and frequently heart wrenching. I remember the first time I had to release a teacher. I vomited a couple times the night before our meeting. It wasn't pretty. But consistency in what you say and how you deliver the message are really important. The following is a great example of what *not* to do.

A colleague superintendent and I jointly shared an employee that we knew had to be dismissed. We decided to take the person, who was a very good and caring person, out to lunch, have a heart-to-heart conversation, and let the person know he/she would not be returning. We agreed that my colleague would buy lunch and I would do the talking. After a very pleasant lunch and what I thought was a wonderful and informative conversation, the person said, "Howard, I am not quite sure what you are saying. Am I being promoted or am I out of a job?" My heart sunk. I replied, "I'm sorry. There are no promotions here." I felt awful and learned a good lesson.

Give the person your time, your eyes, your proper voice intonation, your patience, your honest commitment to listening, your open mind, your quality caring attitude, but, at the end of the day, when "no" is "no," deliver the message with politeness, consistency, and clarity. Don't be wishy-washy. Don't try to be creative by saying "no" in different ways. Be a broken record and say it repeatedly. Then, carefully, slowly begin to stand up, sending the message that the meeting is over. Then, however nicely you can, walk toward the door.

Sometimes you just have to agree to disagree. You can validate the person's concerns, but that's it. And, as my mother would say, we can always do any act with politeness and a show of respect. But "no" is "no" is "no."

Attempt to Eat Healthy.

Does your breakfast consist of birthday treats given to you in the morning by the student-of-the-day or a faculty member, a sweet roll at an early morning meeting, a stop at a vending machine or fast food restaurant on your way to school?

Does your daily exercise routine consist of briskly walking through the halls of the building, running from meeting to meeting or chasing a school bus down the street for a forgotten student? After all aren't you burning those extra calories? Is your current approach to eating meals at work serving you well or do you have a well-stocked desk drawer of antacids and/or other digestive aids?

Unless legally banned, schools can be sanctuaries for vending machines full of chips, pretzels, cookies, popcorn, crackers, and candy. Everyone knows where to find the pop machines, groups or individuals selling boxes of chocolates, rice crispy treats, and donuts. School events such as parent coffees, foundation dinners, faculty potluck luncheons, retirement milestones and fundraisers by the PTA, boosters, or student council usually require food to show cordiality. In many cases, schools can earn some discretionary funds depending on the number of vending machines in the building, so let the vending machines multiply. Wait a minute!

It seems ironic as obesity in children is being discussed and researched on a national level, a school leader may not be setting a good example by taking care of himself or herself by eating properly at school. Time constraints and the stress of the job are two major factors that push school leaders toward unhealthy eating patterns. Some leaders may enter a food coma— a stupor where one is unconsciously grabbing food on the run because one's body is telling you it's time to eat. You don't take the time to sit down for a healthy meal so you are unaware of the health consequences of what you eat. A little cupcake here or a piece of candy there becomes lunch. You resort to a comfort food pattern such as grabbing a bag of chips to make you feel better after some unpleasant experience like a difficult personnel issue or managing an irate parent. Bags of chips chip away at your health and well being causing your body stress.

Being conscious, aware, and satisfied about daily food choices allows you to take control of your body by slowing down and thinking reflectively about food eaten for the day in order to perform productively. There is a difference between eating a sandwich while driving the car or eating calmly in the faculty lounge. Many school leaders unselfishly give up their meals in order to meet the constant demands of school life.

Be mindful of what you are eating and when you are eating. Learn to resist the temptation of eating on the run and don't feel guilty about eating alone at your desk. Find a quiet time during the school day that could be your lunchtime. For me, it was that 15 to 20 minutes after all the lunch periods were over. Bring healthy snacks for yourself if you know it is going to be a hectic day and nibble on them a little at a time if you cannot stop to eat properly. After all aren't we supposed to be modeling healthy eating habits?

While I would be the first to tell you that I am not an expert about diet or nutrition, I can tell you that after I left my central office position at a very large K-12 school district, I lost thirty pounds mainly gained from poor food choices. No, ifs, ands or butts about it!

Avoid Paranoia.

Every month since the early 1980s a group of teachers convenes under the guise of the MMC Monthly Movie Club. The small group of six has not changed and would probably be best described under the rubric of Ralph Kramden and Ed Norton in *The Honeymooners* with Ralph and Ed's revered allegiance to the Royal Order of Raccoons. We have dined at the same place now for twenty-five years, ordering the same two large pizzas and enjoying a beer. We watch action and adventure movies and have a very detailed system of rating movies. We even have an annual Oktoberfest with edited highlights of the best movie scenes. We all have responsibilities from movie critic to secretary. Our jobs never change. I have been vice-president for twenty-five years, never being able to ascend to the presidency. Our president's motto, "No leadership is better than bad leadership" has proven unbeatable. We laugh and joke but also entertain serious debates about schools. Although all of us are retired now from K-12 teaching and administering, schools remain the focus of our conversations.

Before Ken retired we would hear his monthly rendition, bordering on paranoia, about how the principal was out to get rid of him. He was always worried and nervous and our discussions went a long way to let him know that he was an excellent teacher, which he clearly was as evidenced by being tenured, in the district for decades, and having received numerous awards. His job security was not an issue. The camaraderie and conversation went a long way to make him laugh, would get all of us through another month, discuss concerns (real or imagined), and simply relax. Looking at us at these meetings one would never have guessed that this group of rag-tag teachers included several PhDs, a concert pianist, an author of four novels, and a highly successful businessman (post-retirement).

Sometimes we all get very nervous, or even downright scared, and maybe even paranoid. It just feels like somebody is looking over our shoulder all the time. It feels like we are always "walking on eggs." In our profession, we certainly have enough to worry about: high-stakes testing, school violence, unfunded mandates, audits, reform movements, money woes, and Internet safety, to name a few. Then there are your own personal problems be they job security, health problems, or financial challenges. Throw in the world problems of famine, war, poverty, and global warming and maybe we do have enough to get paranoid over. You would think we would all have ticks, ulcers, or twitches by now. Somehow, in the midst of all this, you just have to do your job, the best you can, and remember there is only so much you have control over. You have to create a sense of normalcy. And, above all else, don't get paranoid. It won't help, not in the least.

When I graduated from Northern Illinois University in 1972, I was going to save the world. I certainly didn't even put a dent in my dream. But along the way I did help *my* children as a teacher and *my* employees as a superintendent and principal and maybe I even helped *my* profession a tad.

I stopped trying to save the world and just tried to do my job every day with enthusiasm and to the best of my ability. Don't get me wrong, there were times I was nervous; however, there is a big difference between nervousness and paranoia. I saved being paranoid for the rare and extreme situations. For instance, the time the father of one of my school district employees was distraught because his daughter did not get a promotion that I gave to someone else. He loved his daughter so much that when she cried, he just could not stand it. He made an anonymous phone call to me at work and told me my wife was in a serious car accident and was in the emergency room at a local hospital. Needless to say I was shaking and immediately called the hospital. When the emergency room attendant said my wife was not there, I unsuccessfully tried her cell phone and, subsequently, called other local hospitals. I then called my children, who were adults at the time, and told them to find their mother and stay with her. The whole thing was a hoax. And I was paranoid for quite some time until I figured out who did it. It took me a while but I did solve the case. Probably being a middle school principal for a couple decades gave me the skills to do so. So save paranoia for the extreme circumstances, pray there are none, and learn to live with a little nervousness.

Balance Work and Home, But at Best It's 80/20.

There seems to be a hidden myth or code of silence, if you will, that in our culture family and work revolve in two separate spheres and never "the twain shall meet." Supposedly when we are at work, we are focused on our job, and when we are at home we are focused on our personal life. Some non-educators believe that when we walk out of the school door and head home at the end of the day, our work is done. Those who teach and lead know that work expectations bump, mingle, stir, percolate, and spill all over our personal lives. For a school leader, the relationship of home to work can be 80:20 at best. The reason for this is clear. There are evening meeting expectations, such as fun fairs, concerts, athletic events, practices, and parent, school board, and emergency meetings to name a few. Count the hours each evening grading papers, filling out reports, or writing plans. School work eats into one's personal life and the hours add up. It does not take long before one feels out of balance because of long work hours, amount of time spent at work, demanding job expectations, constant interruptions, and newly assigned tasks so that soon there is a blur between home and work and work and home and back to work again.

So does balance mean cutting back on the amount of work to do at home? Does it mean trying to be more organized and efficient when I am at work? It could. The idea of equal balance between home and work is a fallacy because balance suggests that these two aspects of life (work and home) are opposite and equal positions (picture a fulcrum here) when in reality they slip and slide, blurring one from the other. The real challenge is how to integrate work and home sensibly. One idea that worked for me as an elementary principal was to bring my two small children to work with me on Saturday when I had to catch up on paperwork, reports, and memos. As I worked in my office, I would take out some physical education equipment in the gym and let them play—scooters and basketballs were great fun. Then I would monitor them through the intercom. My son, Peter, still remembers having the gym to himself. (You may need to obtain permission or sign a liability waiver to do this.)

So what does balance in work and home really mean? First, it is not going to be an equal 50/50 balance, so don't become exhausted, frustrated, and stressed out trying to make it so. Next, beware of guilt. Guilt can quietly gnaw at you as you wish you were spending more time at home and conversely can mask itself at home when you know the demands are mounting at work. The nose-to-the grindstone work ethic can produce a quiet guilt, a slow burnout and a mild jealousy toward colleagues who do seem to have a distinct home and personal life. Sometimes there is subtle competition among educators that makes it almost impossible to justify taking time off or leaving work early. The pace of work at school often makes it difficult to carve out time to reflect and make good decisions thus increasing the chances of making mistakes not to mention increasing emotional fatigue. Many educators are afraid and fearful to take time off. Just notice the large number of sick days that educators have accumulated when it comes time to retire. Some educators I know were proud that they never missed a day of work, but I am sure they were missed at home.

Over time, today's right balance might not be tomorrow's right balance. For example, as you become more skillful in the job, moving from a beginning teacher to an experienced teacher, you may not have to spend as much time preparing lessons for the next year as you did in the first year. In the end, it's the balance that works for you, not the balance that works for anyone else. It is what you value and what your priorities are for work and home and how you integrate them.

Buy Term Life Insurance and Hope Your Term Does Not Come Up.

"You've got to ask yourself one question: 'Do I feel lucky?' Well, do ya punk?"

Forget the "punk" part but the rest of Clint Eastwood's question from his movie *Dirty Harry* sure does apply. Do you feel lucky with respect to life? Pretty serious question, perhaps even daunting, but somewhere along the line I think most of us ponder our life expectancy and hope for longevity and a brighter tomorrow.

Some people just do have better luck than others. Some people just happen to be in the right place at the right time and literally fall into something good. As it relates to health some people just seem to have inherited those magnificent genes. I am especially jealous of those with the high metabolism rates who can eat and eat while I seem to put on "their" pounds. I am reminded that for some of us unlucky ones, if it wasn't for bad luck, we would have no luck at all. Or as one of my former school board presidents would say, "If I bought a turkey farm, they'd call off Thanksgiving." Well, whether or not you're lucky enough to have great health or otherwise, it would appear that having term life insurance is a good investment. A note of caution here: I am not a financial planner and can't debate the pros and cons of "whole" versus "term" life insurance. I do know the difference, however, and have primarily purchased term, although I have to admit I think the word "whole" is a lot more comforting.

Many of us receive a term life insurance policy with our jobs and most of us probably pay little attention to it. I didn't either until I delivered a benefit check to a grieving widow of one of my custodians a couple decades ago. No amount of money can ever replace the loss of a loved one, but knowing that the check would provide some financial security certainly made me feel better as an administrator and friend of the family.

Term insurance can represent more than just financial security. It represents good planning and can be symbolic of being a well-prepared and -planned educator. It falls into the same category as having good lesson plans, being prepared for emergency situations, having a roadmap of educational goals and objectives, and, ultimately, knowing that when you go to sleep at night you have done your best to be prepared for the future. In short, it is being responsible to yourself and others.

So buy term life insurance. It should provide you with peace of mind. Of course, we hope your term does not come up.

Discover Your Sense of Humor.

When educators sit down and discuss the qualities they want in a future leader, invariably the discussion turns to the leader having a sense of humor. At first, many leader characteristics are easy to list, such as the person demonstrating good problem solving, listening, or visionary skills. But just like the icing on the cake, at the last moment someone says, "Oh, and by the way, the leader should have a good sense of humor!"

What does that mean? If you don't have a sense of humor can you develop one? Do you have to be funny all the time? Should you begin developing a repertoire of one-liners like David Letterman or Ellen DeGeneres? Let's start with a smile. Everyone has one of those. How can you use your smile to enhance your interactions with people? In some cases, you might even have to practice smiling. Yes, as odd as it might sound, a sincere, genuine smile represents joy and contentment and others pick up on it, respond to it, and may even need that gesture as a boost. Certainly a smile and a hearty laugh are not the same thing, but a smile does show that the weight of the world is not so heavy at any particular moment.

Making light of serious things, clowning around, and pulling pranks are not the same thing as a sense of humor. In fact, some of those actions can seriously backfire. For example, one superintendent thought it was funny during a Back to School Institute Day to show the staff the preemployment videotape of newly hired teachers during their interviews. The videotape was edited by changing the interview questions to reflect different questions such as, "What is your favorite drink or cocktail?", instead of the original question, "What is your homework policy?", while leaving the new teachers' responses the same. With some videotape cutting and splicing, teachers' responses were put on display for all to see. Needless to say, many individuals were offended. The superintendent lost his job. Not so funny.

Humor has a great deal of energy. When people fill a room and are all laughing you can feel it. You can use laughter to your advantage whether you use it to lighten the mood of an oppressive meeting by saying with tongue-in-cheek, "WOW! That was fun!", or diffusing two angry students who are about to engage in a fight, "WOW! I wish I had a camera so you could see your faces right now." Timely and appropriate humor can be an effective tool to improve the working climate of a school. Personally, I believe that a lack of laughter in a school, department, or team can be a sign of trouble. So, as the old adage goes, shouldn't you review your sense of humor and have the last laugh?

Do Crossword Puzzles, Sudoku, Word Jumbles, and More.

Dave Parks is an outstanding custodian and is loved by the students and faculty and is most respected by the school's administration. He gets to work early and does not leave until everything is done. He considers the elementary school building he works in as his property—his school—and his responsibility. He is the "man" and takes care of whatever needs to be done, whether it is making sure the building has heat at six o clock in the morning when it's below zero outside (and knowing what to do immediately if there isn't any) or cleaning up after that child who vomits when you least expect it. There's an old saying, get to know the custodian and the building secretary as they run the place.

At first glance one might not think there is much stress in Dave's school life, but a closer look reveals that when his job is done right, indeed there is stress. From fire alarms to temperature control, from children wanting his recognition to every teacher needing some special attention for their rooms, from the building principal having her priority list to the cooks and clerks having their needs, there most certainly is stress in this man's life. He manages it by knowing his priorities and, everyday, he uses a significant portion of his time during lunch to complete the daily crossword puzzle in the newspaper. And he is really good at it. I never told him that I was embarrassed at how challenging the puzzles were for me when I would look over his shoulder and how easily he would master it day after day. Dave found a niche with that daily crossword puzzle and it gave him a sense of tranquility during a hectic day with hundreds of primary children and several teachers. He exercised his mind, carved out a little peace, and, when done, was ready to go back to the daily grind…relaxed. He was "good to go."

So find your niche with crossword puzzles, Sudoku, word jumbles, or whatever might be a temporary diversion from stress. Determine the time of day that works best for you to do them. For some it may be early morning with your coffee, whereas for others it might be something to do before going to bed. Or for others, like Dave, it will be the respite in a challenging day. In any event, they can be fun, challenging, intellectual, and even collaborative if you choose to do them with a friend (or your students).

To get you started the following one is called, "Education Acronyms." Enjoy!

Across
1. 3.2 million member teacher organization
5. Lacking impulse control
6. Action and processes blueprint for gettin better
7. Enforces federal discrimination laws
9. Fiscal picture profile issued yearly
10. Roadmap for better student conduct
11. Nonnative speaker
12. Assist movement and functional ability
13. Union founded in 1916
14. Provides skills for a job or living

Down
1. Nation's report card test
2. Not reaching milestones at expected times
3. Law prohibiting impairment discrimination
4. Quiet book time in the classroom
5. Statewide accountability system
7. Not first language learner
8. Student progress method administered weekly
11. Famous federal law enacted in 1955
12. Adult school group

Answers to Educational Acronym Puzzle

Across
1. NEA (National Education Association)
5. ADHD (Attention Deficit Hyperactivity Disorder)
6. SIP (School Improvement Plan)
7. EEOC (Equal Employment Opportunity Commission)
9. AFR (Annual Financial Report)
10. BIP (Behavior Intervention Plan)
11. ELL (English Language Learner)
12. PT (Physical Therapy)
13. AFT (American Federation of Teachers)
14. OT (Occupational Therapy)

Down
1. NAEP (National Assessment of Educational Progress)
2. DD (Developmentally Delayed)
3. ADA (Americans with Disabilities Act)
4. SSR (Silent Sustained Reading)
5. AYP (Annual Yearly Progress)
7. ESL (English as a Second Language)
8. CBM (Curriculum Based Measurement)
11. ESEA (Elementary and Secondary Education Act)
12. PTO (Parent Teacher Organization)

Don't Burn the Candle at Both Ends

Recently I watched an online video in a section nicknamed *Geek Science* (http://www.flixxy.com/candle-physics). It showed a 9¼-inch taper candle with a wick at both ends being removed from a candle box. A hand appeared, measured the candle with a ruler, and put a long, thick (possibly darning) needle through the exact center of the candle. Next the hand placed the candle on top of two identical short, wide-mouthed glasses, perfectly balanced on both sides by the needle. Then the hand lit both ends of the candle. For a second nothing happened, but as the candle burned evenly toward the middle, one end of the candle rose wildly while the other lowered to counterbalance. Picture a teeter-totter here. Then the other end rose wildly and the opposite end lowered to counterbalance. To my surprise, the candle remained balanced between the two glasses and did not fall off. The candle's movement slowed and eventually stopped. As both ends of the candle continued to burn toward the middle, the extreme, seesaw process happened again: one end of the lit candle went wildly up almost straight vertical to the glass, while the other end dropped to the base of the glass to compensate and counterbalance. Then the video abruptly ended.

This vivid, silent visual clearly reminded me that the experimental candle could be a symbol of a school leader's body. Like the candle being lit at both ends, a school leader's day may resemble the routine of getting little sleep or rest, staying up late and getting up early; physically, our bodies must react. Just like the wild up-and-down candle, our bodies react toward extreme behavior trying to resolve the imbalance of sleep and work. And what usually comes out is a cranky, moody, and tired school leader who has exhausted his or her energies as the pace of the school day marches on.

There are individuals who say, "Well, I am a person who doesn't need much sleep, don't worry about me. I always look this way." I say, this might be a candidate for the "Burned Out Leader Club." Look for dark circles and squinty and puffy eyes. Once in a while don't be afraid to "call it a day," even though your work setting enjoys seeing you there day and night. Find and protect a respite in the week so as to maintain a healthy balance for your body and life.

Exercise Regularly.

You know you should. You know how you feel when you don't. You know what the research says about stress and the job, and yet when it comes to exercise, it can easily be the last thing on the "School Leader To-Do List," and in some cases, it may never appear on a list at all. Someone once said, "Do you know why school leaders have such big chairs? So they can fit into them!" We read about obesity and the need to provide more physical activity for students in schools, to inspect lunch menus for fats, fillers, and fast food in an attempt to keep kids healthy, but what should school leaders be modeling and doing concerning their health?

Exercise is a primary coping resource in the body—a therapy for reducing negative energy, stress, and pressure. It's like that Green Hulk life-size punching bag that kids would hit and it would bounce right back. Exercise can help the body after its been punched during the day with hassles, demands, and pressures. It can recover and regroup by bouncing back if given the time to exercise. Whether you play tennis and hit the ball around or walk miles on a treadmill, physical engagement appears to release feelings of anger and pressure in a constructive, healthy, and acceptable way after it has accumulated. Incidentally, walking through the halls and into classrooms does not count as regular exercise during the day; however, walking around the perimeter of the building to equal a mile or more would.

Some exercises, such as jogging, swimming, cross-country skiing, and bicycling, can put an individual into a meditative state. Possibly it is the repetition of motion that soothes the mind and alters one's perceptions that leads an individual into a state of calmness and tranquility. It's like being on a mental vacation for some individuals or in a trance. Some leaders use a morning run to organize their day or review an issue or problem solve. Or possibly it is the sweating when lifting weights that cleanses and contributes to the body's peacefulness. Whatever it is, exercise refreshes and recharges the body to go back "into the ring" and face another day.

Find a form of exercise that you enjoy. If you like to run, then run. If you hate running and/or have bad knees, then find something else and do it on a regular basis. Busy school leaders must find the time to exercise and might do so by squeezing it in before they go home by organizing an in-school aerobics class, or using the school facilities and equipment with a group of faculty friends. Many school leaders enjoy starting their day with a brisk walk or run. When exercise during the day does not work, try buying a treadmill and using it while watching the news. Frequent physical activity helps reduce stress overload. Remember that the "Weekend Warrior Exerciser" is not the goal. The goal is a commitment to a regular workout routine.

Facilitate a Common Sense Solution.

Published in 1776, Thomas Paine's *Common Sense* rallied support for the Revolutionary War. Paine's numerous positions opposing British rule were straightforward, pointed, and, ultimately, made good "common sense" to the colonists. If we can wage war and become an independent United States of America using *Common Sense* as a platform, shouldn't we be able to solve problems in our day-to-day lives using "common sense?" Shouldn't that be relatively easy?

Well, for starters, don't you wonder what happened to common sense when events like the following happen?

Children come to school in ice-cold weather wearing t-shirts.
Students of all ages come to school sick with high temperatures and vomiting.

- A student decides to experiment with a pencil and pushes it up his nose.
- A student is caught cheating and calls his parents who call their lawyer who calls you before you are even aware that a problem exists.
- A parent challenges the validity and integrity of a school's report card system, being convinced that all his child's grades have been reported incorrectly (too low, of course).
- A school's staff spends their professional development day at the racetrack.
- A teacher duct tapes a child's mouth.
- An administrator serves sexually explicit pasta to the faculty on the first day of school.

During the course of your work, have you ever felt like saying any of the following (not just silently to yourself but out loud and directly to a person's face)?

- "What happened to your common sense?"
- "What were you thinking?"
- "What planet are you from anyway?"
- "Were you dropped at an early age?"
- "Please just go away and come back when you can think like a normal person."
- "Do you have a screw loose or something?"

Can we really have common sense when we live in a pluralistic and diverse society? Can we really have common sense when we, as a teaching community strive, for differentiated instruction, individualized learning, and employ so many curriculum modifications? Can we have common sense when every child is sacred to his or her parents? The answer is *yes*.

When faced with strong differences of opinion, or for that matter, absurdity, sometimes I found it helpful to say, "Let's just try and use some common sense here." Then I tried to depersonalize the problem by shifting from second person conversations to third person conversations. Instead of saying "you" or "your child," I moved to the third person, such as, "The problem we are addressing is...." For example, within the realm of discipline problems requiring suspensions where every child seems to have a lawyer these days, my goal was to get the parent to say, "Well, it sounds like my child should be suspended." Obviously, that is very hard to do, but it is a noble goal and in many cases, attainable. You have to give people the facts and you need to take the time to get as many of them that will surface. Then slowly let the parents come to a conclusion. Hopefully, you have led them there and not just told them. I would frequently give examples without student names of similar problems and share how they were resolved and how those resolutions balanced with staff and community expectations. I might say, "I understand what you are saying but the couple of times this year when a student was disrespectful with a teacher I had to follow through with our discipline code. It says the student is to be suspended. That is what is expected of *schools* to do." Of course, it does not always work, but it does in many cases.

Listen and be respectful to positions, but remember that, in the end, there is "common sense" out there and the vast majority of those you work with, associate with, report to, and who live in the community, if given the same situation, would come to the same or a similar conclusion. Our legal system provides for a provision known as the "reasonable man" theory. Reasonableness is an attribute that is discernible and quantifiable. Just practice it.

So be reasonable, rational, sound-minded, and employ just good old plain common sense. You will be respected for it and in the end people will say you did the only thing you could and *it made sense*.

Find a Compadre.

Working on my dissertation at Northwestern University in 1982 necessitated my interviewing dozens of superintendents. The vast majority of them allotted me whatever time was needed to complete the survey, but a few of them, like Paul Jung, William Attea, and Homer Harvey, went way above and beyond. They gave me hours of their precious time and provided insights that went much further than the needed requirement for the interview. They got personal and almost preacher-like. In today's terms, they would be known as mentors and/or coaches. Within their circle of colleagues these people were well respected and known as outstanding superintendents. They were busy, very busy, people, but what made them special was that they cared deeply about our profession and took the time with everybody in their path to better our profession.

Paul Jung was such a wonderful human being. He not only served as an inspiring superintendent of two school districts, but also after retirement went on to serve as mayor of one of his communities. He was known for his kind heart and his frequent visits to the police and fire department with donuts. He also served as president of the American Association of School Administrators.

After I conducted my interview with Paul, he continued to talk with me for about three hours, sharing his suggestions for successful school administration and life. He listened to me, responded, and always had some nugget of wisdom to impart. He spoke of the loneliness of the superintendency, constant nature of problem solving, and stress on the job, and more. He then offered a piece of advice I have never forgotten: "Find a compadre." It was stated straightforward and with eyes glaring as if it were to be the most important piece of information he would impart. He then went on to say *not* your spouse or significant other and *not* someone you supervise or vice-versa. But a friend who will understand you, listen to you, and provide support to you on an ongoing basis and be there during challenging times. Someone who will understand the nature of a demanding job and be available on a regular basis to have a conversation with. Someone you trust and someone who can provide you with an outlet from the stressful days we all face in education. Someone who will meet you for breakfast, lunch, or dinner, or who will lift a beer (or beverage of your choice) with you and smile. Someone who is nonjudgmental and who has a very good sense of humor. Most importantly, someone who will be there for you. Find a compadre and do it while you still have your sanity.

Get Everyone Involved Rather Than Upset.

The principal has erred and the master schedule needs changing on the first day of school.

A teacher does not prepare report card grades on time.

A parent challenges a teacher's teaching methods.

A child is harassed going home from school.

A team of teachers is not using the adopted textbook with their students.

The bus traffic at school is a tangled mess.

Evening school events leave the hallway and building messy for the next day.

Graffiti keeps reappearing on walls.

Aggravating, annoying daily situations that take on a life of their own can quickly wear a school leader down. Sometimes bagging at the grocery store looks better than coming to school on any particular day. It is easy to lash out, get upset, let anger build up, say things you don't mean and regret them later.

But the leader must champion involvement and provide opportunity for people to become engaged in school conflicts, thus reducing the stress of others and that of the leader. The hard work of leadership includes exploring alternatives to situations, staying cool and focused, and facilitating the process of looking for solutions. Simple comments, such as, "What can I do to help you with that report?", are all a teacher may need in order to redo the work instead of reading the "riot act" to someone who already knows the deadline has been missed. Students may have constructive ideas on how to solve their own problems when alternatives are placed before them as in peer-mediation councils, face-to-face discussions, and contracts about alternatives. In my experience, parents may need to be invited to school multiple times and in multiple ways to get them involved.

At the beginning of each school year, when I first met with parents, I said, "Being involved in your child's school and education is not an option any more. The job of educating a child is so complex that the school needs everyone's help. Here is what you can do to help...and there are workshops to assist you being offered at school on....What can we do to help you?" Informational packets to parents at the beginning of the school year contained lists of ways to volunteer at school and/or help at home, and ways that everyone could be involved together. New ideas were always welcomed and parent groups at school addressed specific topics they wanted to discuss at their meeting.

Teachers also had opportunities to receive small amounts of money through mini and seed grants to form study groups about issues and problems that concerned them and their school. The money used paid for time spent studying the issue in depth in order to find local solutions and involved in the process teachers who ultimately presented their findings to their colleagues.

Another example is plain, open, and honest conversation—"coffees," talks with the leader once a month to hear concerns from and offer feedback among all stakeholders in the school community. Rather than harboring problems, fostering conflicts, and then letting them explode, teachers, parents, and students can be offered opportunities to become active, involved, problem solvers when the leader offers problem-solving opportunities.

Learn to Live with a Full Plate.

You come into your office early to get a head start on the day. As you sit at your desk you click on your email and notice you have forty-five that are unread from the day before. Where did they come from? They must have multiplied in cyberspace. As you scroll through them, one in particular catches your eye and you read about a mini crisis that needs immediate attention. You compose a response but it is not finished when a teacher knocks on your door to remind you that she is leaving work at lunch today and do you have a substitute lined up. You are not sure. A parent stands outside your office asking to talk to you about her child's grades and progress reports. You tell the parent you will talk with her immediately after you check about the sub. You make a quick call to confirm the sub and find out everything is in order. You email the teacher that everything is okay for the afternoon absence. You invite the parent into your office, she takes a seat and tells you about the problem she is having in the neighborhood with students from the school that are affecting her child's grades. You listen intently but your phone is ringing. The morning bell rings and you realize the school day has just begun.

In a matter of minutes the above leader will be on overload as a result of the number of interactions that are multiplying and mounting. The overload might be in the form of information overload (emails and conversations), data overload (test results and analysis), demand overload (everyone asking for something and the promises made), regulation overload (procedural clutter, structural processes, and hoop jumping), or brain overload (too much to do and too little time). Fallout from overload can hinder your productivity, increase your mistakes and impact your attitude within a few minutes if not managed.

Managing disruptions and distractions by how and when you respond to them are crucial to reducing your stress. Your plate is always full and how you empty it depends on careful decision making. Here are some suggestions: First, avoid checking email first thing in the day. Gluing yourself to the computer can be a full-time job in itself and can take you away from the people who need you most—the students. Second, prioritize your work by staying focused on your chosen items and following through with tasks so that you see quality work completion. Avoid bouncing from task to task, or if you find yourself doing that, readjust your priorities. Finally, simplify, like Michael Jordan who when asked how he met his goal of thirty-two points a game responded that he broke the game into four quarters challenging himself to score eight points in each one, thus meeting his final goal. (McCormack, 2000). So relax, rebound, and resolve that you can live with a full plate.

Leave Your Ego at the Front Door.

The following humorous story may or may not be true.

A famous athlete was vacationing with his wife and three children in a quaint New England town. They had come a long distance to have a relaxing and quiet weekend get away. The family decided to take in an afternoon movie at the local theater. Arriving a few minutes late, they noticed the movie had not started. They were relieved. As they walked down the aisle, the small crowd of twenty-five people all stood up on their feet and started clapping and welcoming them. The star athlete immediately waved to the crowd and responded, "I had no idea you knew I was in town. Thank you for this warm welcome." A member of the audience responded, "What are you talking about? The movie can't start until thirty people are here!"

Predisposition, or perceptual set as we learned in our Psychology 101 class, plays a major role in how we view life and "take it all in." For some people in the world, it is the money that "gets to them." For others it's the stardom. For others it's the success. For others it's that title or advanced degree. For others it's the power. For others it's their position. And for others, well, they just seem to be born that way. What way? Well, their first instinct is to relate all the world's incoming information through an egocentric self-centered lens—"me first," "I'm special," and "I am just so important." In other words, "How does this affect me, my reputation, and my ego?" The person tends to be hell bent on being important and letting us know it. The person can become argumentative or, better yet, develop a reputation that he or she is not worth talking to because the conversation will go nowhere like hitting a brick wall. The person will just get defensive. Or better yet, you had best be careful because the person will hold it against you (and your children).

Hopefully most of what we do in our profession is for the betterment of our profession—for our students. If that is true doesn't it make sense to view information through a prism of students first? Drop the attitude, drop the me-first, don't dominate conversations, don't be defensive, don't become argumentative and decline being the devil's advocate, and, most importantly, don't take it personal, because it's not. It's so much healthier to filter conversations on their merit and just leave your ego at the front door.

It's not about you; it's about the system. It's about making your school a better place. Maybe it's true what people say about me that I have no ego at all. And maybe it's true that that's not healthy either. But I will tell you that leaving your ego at the front door will earn you the reputation of being a listener, communicator, door opener, down to earth, and child advocate.

Rodney Dangerfield would say, "I don't get no respect." You will, if your ego stays at the front door. And with it will come an atmosphere that will make your school a better place. And it won't be perfect. I am reminded of one of my parents with whom I worked so hard to develop a close relationship. I listened to her, was attentive, never got upset, and always tried to pluck those nuggets from our conversation that would be valuable. One year, on the last day of school, after listening to a barrage of "stuff," I said, "You know Mrs. _____, I am really trying hard to listen and support you." She responded, "Well, Howard, you're just going to have to try harder." I did. I leave my ego at the front door and feel much better for having done so.

Let "It" Go.

"Dr. Bultinck the White House is on the phone for you."

"Sure they are, just tell the president I am a little busy right now."

"No, I am serious. The White House *is* on the line. She says it is the Office of the Social Secretary. She is holding on line one."

Have you ever felt like you were having an "out-of-body" experience or someone was playing a really good prank on you but you just couldn't figure out who was doing it? That is exactly how I felt when this phone call came through. The White House was on the line and inviting my middle school choral singing group, *EagleSong,* to perform there during the Christmas season. It was truly an amazing trip, topped off by a performance for and personal audience with First Lady Hillary Clinton. We sang our best for her (par rum pa pum pum, rum pa pum pum—a little holiday humor here) and she was very pleasant, fixated on the children, and complimentary about our performance. It was a Christmas miracle for me and I truly did feel that I was having an "out-of-body" experience. Seeing the White House, the White House Christmas tree, the adrenaline rush watching the children perform, the First Lady…amazing.

After *EagleSong* had the opportunity to sing at the White House, they led off Macy's Thanksgiving Day Parade as part of a larger group entitled *America Sings.* I was home that Thanksgiving Day morning and as I peeled potatoes at the kitchen table and witnessed my children kick off the parade on TV, I remember thinking, "It just doesn't get any better than this." What was truly amazing was less the events than the fact that the middle school chorus was created and taught by a volunteer. Yes, that's right, a volunteer. A man who gave countless hours every day for well over a decade to allow any child, yep, no cuts, to sing and become the best they could be. It was an example of giving at its finest.

Gary Fry, assisted by his wife, Carol, is internationally known for his musical genius. He believes in giving back and would barely accept a "Thank You" for all his work. He was an example of what the world could really be like if everyone cared and volunteered. He loved the children and thoroughly enjoyed watching them perform. He knew each and every one of them as well as any great teacher. After singing during halftime at National Football League games, performing in numerous concerts with the Chicago Symphony Orchestra, and even singing at the United Nations, we were invited back to the White House. Needless to say it was a principal's dream—a superior program, supported by the school's administration, community, and staff, all for the benefit of the children. One year would just roll into the next.

And then one day it ended. I could see it coming for quite some time. For a variety of reasons, it was time for Gary to move on to a different project that would require a great deal of his time. It was so hard for me to let go. I stayed awake nights for countless weeks trying to figure out a way to allow the program to continue. I brainstormed with Gary, my board members, and others. But, alas, to no avail. Gary was the kind of man that is rare. He was a volunteer for volunteerism's sake. He was one in a million. And he was gone.

Sometimes in life you just have to let go. The thing you don't have any control over—let *it* go. The thing you can't influence—let *it* go. Your need to help when help is not possible—let *it* go. The wishful thinking of a project that is absolutely dead in the water—let *it* go. The nagging feeling that if you just worked harder when you are already working too much—let *it* go. Your constant concern over the parent who just won't let up on you—let *it* go. Remember Freddie Hart's song lyrics, "Please release me, let me go...." Sometimes you just have to release yourself and let go, if not only for your health's sake. You just have to allow yourself the liberty of saying goodbye. Don't get me wrong, most things are worth fighting for, even worrying about, but in the end there will be some things that you will not be able to salvage for one reason or another. *It* may be financially impossible, logistically inconceivable, physically impractical or politically suicidal. And, for your sake, just let your *it* go. You will be healthier for doing so and have more energy and time for your next challenge, which, in our profession, is lurking right around the corner.

Live with a Little Loneliness.

Rare is the person who is never lonely. Students, teachers, and school leaders can all experience loneliness in the work place at some time or another. It is normal. A school leader who is never around, whose door is always closed, and who is never accessible to the school community when needed, can be described as a "contrived loner." This is a choice to be unavailable to those who are in need—a type of separation, if you will, that is unhealthy and toxic to the school.

Unpopular decisions can also produce loneliness for the school leader. If decisions are deemed unfair, excessive, unreasonable, or unethical, others may choose not to follow. Ultimately, the quality of the followership is reduced and so is the success of the leader.

When I was a seventh and eighth grade language arts teacher, I was asked to substitute for my principal who was going to have surgery. Although we all assumed that my stay in the office would be for one or two weeks, in reality weeks became months as he experienced postsurgical complications. Trying to keep things in order from day to day soon came to halt. As time went by important decisions had to be made, teachers needed to be evaluated, and students' needs had to be met. My position as substitute principal quickly became interim principal and with it a change in how my colleagues and teammates perceived me. Conversations changed when I entered the faculty lounge, as well as those invitations to have a drink after school on Friday with my colleagues. All in all, I did feel lonely and was in a holding pattern waiting for my boss to return. After six months he did return, but many subtle changes had already taken place. I became uncomfortable going back to being a classroom teacher and my colleagues had trouble welcoming me back. I had experienced success in the principal's office and knew I could do the work. The loneliness I experienced going from a teaching position to an administrative position in my school actually turned out to be a catalyst to begin my search for my first principalship which I found the following school year.

At times a school leader's position is a lonely one. Live with it.

Schedule an Annual Physical Exam Whether or Not You Think You Need One.

At the age of thirty-three I became a school superintendent. The school board had experienced significant health issues with the prior superintendent and, as such, built into my contract a requirement to have an annual physical exam. When I first saw this I was not pleased, even though they would pay the amount my insurance did not. It would take time away from my job. Time that was needed for a challenging position in a small district that combined superintendent with principal and business manager. It was wasted time because I was in great shape (just ask me, right?). I was young, exercising somewhat, and had no reason to carve out unneeded time for a routine bloodletting. As an aside, I also am not fond of needles! So I decided to make the appointment on the day after Thanksgiving because it was a day off and an easy one to remember every year. Eventually I changed the date of the annual physical exam— turkey, mashed potatoes, gravy, and desserts over time made this day a pretty stupid choice for a weigh-in. But life went on and over a couple decades I did learn a few things.

I learned that an annual physical is like a life insurance policy. It somewhat insures that your health continues to be good or may give you an unknowing and unsuspected finding that can be treated if detected in its early stages. It provides a time for you to reflect on your overall health and make available to you detailed feedback on everything from your cholesterol level and blood pressure to incremental changes in your overall body chemistry. As a couple things were remedied in my case, I came to look forward to the yearly event because upon receiving positive results I felt ready to roll for another year. I felt relatively "insured" that the hard work and labor-intensive efforts of my job would go uninterrupted for another year. I felt relatively assured that my family would see me a bit and probably not be collecting on my life insurance. In sum I had a better mental outlook and frame of mind and reference for the next twelve months because I received a clean bill of health. There is much to be said for preventative medicine, routine health screenings, and getting that annual flu shot. This is probably why many insurance companies will pay for a physical exam at least once every two years.

So, schedule your annual physical exam even if you are young and in great health or don't think you need one. It is worth the time, effort, and expense to receive that annual report. It has been said, "If you have your health, you have everything."

Suck It Up on the Tough Days.

Every job, occupation and profession has challenges and tough days. So it goes without saying that school leaders face significant challenges and have tough days. There are daily emergencies, frustrations, irritations, and aggravations that can accumulate and cause stress and wear down even the most optimistic and resilient leader. You know it is a tough day when...

teachers lose their jobs due to a reduction in force (RIF).

budget dollars disappear earlier than the end of the fiscal school year.

the home life of a child is not worth going home to.

the buses run late.

a student is missing.

snow, sleet, and ice close school.

a colleague dies.

a student brings a weapon to school (in my case a kindergartner brought a butcher knife for show and tell).

there is a shortage of subs and even the subs are calling in sick.

The above list is only a speck in the universe of challenges that a school leader faces. Usually something unique and potentially tough will happen every day at school as no two days (just like teaching) are ever the same or predictable. There will be things that you don't want to do and events that go wrong. Succeeding in our work is not always convenient, scheduled, or obvious. Because there are always surprises associated with the school day, suck it up, deal with it, handle it, and move on. Accept the challenges as yours and with it experience the satisfaction that comes from good decision making. Don't be afraid to tell yourself "good job" or "that wasn't so bad" because in retrospect you have proven to others and yourself that you can do the job. Learn to enjoy the tough days and keep in mind that in a week or two no one will probably remember what happened (exclude tragedies here) because time is on your side. But most of all take a deep breath, relax at home, get ready for tomorrow, and remember how lucky you are to be working with children.

Try Not to Be Too Hard on Yourself.

I remember a couple decades ago when my sister, Barbara, became a Kindergarten teacher. She was running herself ragged trying to do everything right for *her* children. One day she asked me, "How does one find the time to do all the right things for students? How does one find all the time to individualize (now differentiate) lesson plans, let alone prepare for parent–teacher conferences and do the daily bureaucratic requests?" I remember simply saying, "There isn't enough time. You have to set a time limit (of course, I suggested working 12-hour days and carving out weekend time too) and live with it." She continued to be too hard on herself for not doing all the things she thought she should.

There is an endless supply of monthly articles, magazines, books, and self-help guides for personal improvement. We have health clubs, personal trainers, life coaches, nutritionists, and dieticians for just these types of things. Most of us want to improve our efficiency, our lives, our work, our health, and maybe even our looks. Many of us probably have that New Year's resolution we are still working on. Incremental improvement is good, but some of us—the real go-getters—push ourselves too hard. And we can be much harder on ourselves than anyone else ever would be.

The following story illustrates how something new, better, and creative came from being hard on myself. I learned something very interesting about teachers, and people in general for that matter, out of sheer desperation. For more than a decade I served as superintendent, principal, and business manager of a small school district. It was a real challenge to survive every day and feel like I was doing a good job at anything. Teacher evaluations and classroom teaching observations are the most critical components of effective clinical supervision. But there were so many teachers to observe and so little time. I didn't use a simple trait checklist. I conducted classroom observations, took script notes, and wrote all the classroom observations from scratch. They were so tedious and time-consuming, especially trying to individualize and personalize each one. But that was what a principal is supposed to do. To survive, I eventually migrated to videotaping the teacher and reviewing the videotape before the write-ups. The teachers asked to see the tapes. I said sure, "Help yourself." Then I began giving the teachers the tapes and asking them to evaluate themselves and report back to me before I said or did anything.

A funny thing happened on the way to survival. Because it was an atmosphere of trust, the staff was so much harder on themselves than I ever would have been. They had more suggestions for improvement than I could shake a stick at. Their write-ups were excellent and modeled excellent writing skills. Previously, I would select several items that were commendable and one or two areas for improvement. The staff would have a litany of things for improvement. They were so tough on themselves. They were also quite funny. One teacher told me that the videotape changed her life. After seeing it she went on a diet and lost twenty pounds. I learned from that to tell everyone to watch the tape twice—once just to see how one looked and the second time to see how the lesson went. Another teacher told me that her husband walked by as she was watching the tape. He sat down next to her and said, "You know, hon, you really are a great teacher." She also said she made popcorn before viewing the video. I had so much practice videotaping teachers, I thought weddings and bar mitzvahs were in my future. I learned to zoom in on specific aspects of classroom teaching, student interactions, and student work products. I learned to do a global scan, as well as migrate from one student to another student after about five seconds. I learned to scan the entire classroom for bulletin boards, mandatory emergency notices, and the classroom environment. In the end, the teacher wound up with a video yearbook of her class and, as years went by, the teacher would have tapes to make year-to-year comparisons as well as vignettes to view during one's career progression. This was a good way to reduce my desperate feeling of the time crunch involved in teacher evaluations.

Today's teacher supervision systems vary from goal setting, trait checklist, and narratives to 360-degree feedback. So many choices and so little time. We don't need perfectionism in our work. Look what happens to children and adults who have those tendencies. We see ulcers, twitches, and so on. But let's try to get a little better every day and not be too hard on ourselves along the way. As our mother would say, "everything in moderation."

Use Sunday Evenings to Prepare for the Week.

I used to tell my three children that they better find a life's profession that they enjoy, like I did, otherwise they would be really challenged every day to "rise and shine." I would tell them that their life, thoughts, feelings, and actions would be greatly impacted by daily work experience. I would throw out that old line, "find something you love to do and you will never work another day in your life." Yeah, right. Although we may feel that we are contributing to humanity through our profession, the name of the game is still challenging and very, very stressful.

I am ever so jealous of those teachers and administrators whose classrooms and offices are so pristine. You know the ones whose every bulletin board is up-to-date and beautiful, all papers are graded, and the desk has "show space" with very few things on it. Then you have the flip side—me. Once in a while I would stop in my tracks, look at my classroom or office, and say, "Whoa, I gotta get organized; I gotta clean this mess up; it's outta control."

Being organized in your classroom and office is one thing, but having a game plan for the week is even more important. Knowing what you need to accomplish and having a roadmap for doing so can greatly reduce your stress and make you feel much more accomplished at week's end. As you complete items you will feel good crossing them off your list. Early on in my career I learned to take Sunday evening and reflect on the previous week, think about my long-term goals, and carefully craft a plan for the upcoming week. I would review all my plans and appointments and look at everything from what events would be more challenging and stressful than others to how much sleep I could expect to get every night. By doing so not only did I feel prepared for what I knew was coming but also I felt somewhat prepared for the unexpected. That's right. I felt like I could handle the unexpected because I knew what was expected. A colleague superintendent once told me that when he was struggling with a nationwide media problem on hazing, it just sucked the life and fun out of the job. He was a master at handling problems and it finally did go away. Even if you do not face the media or tackle a serious problem, being well armed going into the week can get you ready for whatever comes your way. Whether it is a major problem that goes on for weeks, or a short-term challenge like a school closing for inclement weather, or an irate parent complaining about you to your supervisor, an hour or two on a Sunday night is well worth the investment to "feel" organized, "feel" prepared, and "feel" like you know what lies ahead.

Guadalupe Martinez, an experienced principal and my graduate student, even cooks all her meals on Sunday night for the week. Now that's prepared! Use that Sunday night to create your flight plan; it will help you navigate what is typical in our profession—a very, very long week.

When You Wake Up Tired, Remember at Least You Woke Up.

Your morning alarm clock sounds off and hits you like a lead balloon. You whack the snooze button a couple times but it does not come close to helping. Let's face it, you're exhausted. It's Friday morning, the end of a very long week and a very long month that saw you struggling to grade papers, chair meetings, and pleasantly greet parents at an open house—an open house where you tried to make a good impression while fending off those needy parents who wanted detailed answers to questions about their children that should have been reserved for parent–teacher conferences. It was exhausting; then you bumped into one of your neighbors who commented, tongue-in-cheek, how easy teachers have it with those short days and ever-so-long summer vacations. You are so tired that even the smell of freshly brewed coffee can't get you jump-started. You also know how easy today will be—being a Friday and all...*not*! I am reminded of the joke about the mother demanding that her son get out of bed and go to school. She doesn't care how tired he is and prods him numerous times until she insists upon her obedience. When he asks her why he has to go to school she responds: "Because you are the principal!"

Well guess what—you have to go to school, too. And you know what else? No matter how exhausted you are at least you woke up. That's right. Life is sometimes that simple. Each day is a gift and you should be thankful for it and the contribution you can make to our profession. During the course of our careers, if you live long enough, you will more than likely experience the death of a relative, a friend, or a loved one. In the school setting perhaps the death of a parent or relative of a student, or, as I have seen, even the death of a student. Perhaps even the tragic death of a student who takes his or her own life or a life that is taken innocently by a stray bullet or an act of God. In any event, it is awful. It is devastating. It is so sad and sometimes depressing that you ask yourself how or why this could have happened.

Then there are success stories, too. Stories like Becca who was diagnosed with cancer in sixth grade. Her father, a doctor, came and shared her story with all her classmates. He told them what would happen next—the treatment, the radiation and chemotherapy, and, hopefully, the cure. You could not hear a pin drop as he spoke. He spoke of the treatments, hair loss, and more. Her mother made her a hat to wear to school every day with a braid dangling down the back to give the appearance of it being Becca's hair. Other than the hat, Becca would not stand out in school during her treatments. The braid, made from her mother's hair, was beautiful and so symbolic. And life went on. Becca got better and continues to this day to be a beautiful, bright and outstanding student—and cancer free.

There are all kinds of sad stories that engulf our lives. But whatever you grapple with in yours, just remember that in life's tough times put everything on the awful scale. Really, how bad is it? Judge fairly, keep things in perspective and remember, even on the exhausting days, to be thankful because yes, indeed, you did wake up.

4
On Staying Alive

Current administrative turnover trends, as reflected in local, state, and national statistics, reveal a school leader revolving door—a door few would choose to get stuck in. Although the school system will survive, leaving school leadership positions early is fraught with problems for both the departing school leader and for all remaining school stakeholders. This chapter will assist you in creating the power of "staying put" in your job by making the most of your leadership and interpersonal skills, work ethic, planning and organization skills, creative thinking abilities, expertise in interpretation of data, and technology talents.

According to Richard Mihans (2008, p. 762), "The numbers are in and they are not rosy." Mihans is referring to the high teacher attrition rates in the twenty-first century. Another resource, www.retainingteachers.com, references the U.S. Bureau of Labor Statistics (U.S. Department of Labor, 2006), which states, "Teachers hold 3.8 million jobs in elementary and secondary U.S. public and private schools, representing approximately 4% of the total civilian workforce." As this website discusses, according to the National Commission on Teaching and America's Future (2003, p.1), "Despite the number of newly hired teachers, in an average school year, approximately 1,000 teachers quit each school day and on an average school day an additional 1,000 teachers migrate from one school to another. On average, a third of newly hired teachers leave during their first three years; almost half leave during the first five years."

Cynthia Kopkowski, (2008) reports that "Nationally, the average turnover for all teachers is 17 percent, and in urban school districts specifically, the number jumps to 20 percent, according to the National Center for Education Statistics. The National Commission on Teaching and America's Future proffers starker numbers, estimating that one-third of all new teachers leave after three years, and 46 percent are gone within five years." She continues by stating, "Their departure through what researchers call the 'revolving door' that's spinning ever faster—the Commission estimates teacher attrition has grown by 50 percent over the past 15 years—costs roughly $7 billion a year, as districts and states recruit, hire, and try to retain new teachers."

But guess what? The high rate of teacher turnover is because of dissatisfaction with so many aspects of the job, such as teacher compensation, perceived lack of administrator support, inadequate working conditions, and disappearance of professional autonomy (Mihans, 2008). Our experience would suggest additional reasons, including lack of professional respect, classroom management issues, safety concerns, parental pressures, students with attorneys, inadequate resources such as textbooks and supplemental materials to use in teaching, shortage of technology and the related unreliable servicing of what technology there is, and increased accountability as a result of high-stakes testing with the standards-based reform movement and the *No Child Left Behind Act*.

And it is not just teachers who are turning over; it is administrators as well. Faced with the daunting challenges and responsibility for student achievement and test scores, building relationships with administrators and school boards, legal system complexities, dealing with special interest groups, managing school politics, and annual budget challenges, administrators seek or are required to obtain new jobs. Facets of school administration can suck the life out of the enjoyment that one looks for when working with students on a daily basis.

The National Association of Elementary School Principals (NAESP) has conducted surveys of principals every ten years for eight decades. Daud and Keller (1998, p. 11) report based on the seventh survey that "The 1998 study of the K-8 Principal suggests that the principal's role has become increasingly diverse and complex, and that the 42 percent turnover in the principalship during the last ten years is likely to continue into the next decade." The principals' traditional roles in staff supervision, student discipline/management, and student interaction were altered to include increased responsibilities in areas such as marketing their schools, political involvement for financial support, increased involvement with social service agencies for student needs, site-based council work, and fiscal decision making. Principals reported increased influence with respect to school decisions and decreased authority to make such decisions. This was especially true when it came to things that went wrong.

At the time of writing this book, NAESP was in the process of completing its eighth study in this series. It has been shared with us that the data indicate that the responses to the current survey (2008) found that 50% of the respondents state they have been in the principalship for less than ten years. The turnover (not retirement) is estimated to be greater than 50% over the next ten years (NAESP Leadership Academy, 2008).

Principal turnover is continuous and inevitable. Elissa Gootman's article in the *New York Times* (May 22, 2006), "Heavy Turnover in New York's Principal Ranks," reports that more than 50% of New York City public school principals during the last five years have left their jobs. The article continues to state that it is pressure from above and a new scrutiny of student performance that cause senior principals to give up in frustration; demographics are also playing a role (http://www.nytimes.com/2006/05/22nyregion/22principals.htm).

Superintendent turnovers fare even worse. *The State of the American School Superintendency, A Mid-Decade Study* (Glass & Franceschini, 2007) provides a wealth of data with respect to school superintendents. One piece of data indicates that the mean number of years served in the current superintendency is estimated to be 5.5, with the median estimated to be 5.7 years. The article reports, "Superintendent tenure rates are often confused with turnover rates. Tenure rates traditionally have hovered around 6 years, but state turnover rates appearing in media stories often claim that 20% or 25% of a state's superintendents have turned over in a given year. It is not commonly understood that when a superintendent retires or leaves a district, two superintendent positions are affected. The first is the one vacated by the retiring superintendent and the second by the superintendent leaving a trailing district fill the vacated position."

The number of years served by school superintendents in their last superintendency revealed the following data:

Not applicable: 50.2% (new or interim superintendents)
1–5 years: 28.0%
6–9 years: 14.1%
10+ years: 7.6%

The turnover rates for large school districts become even more disconcerting. Glass and Franceschini (2007) state, "A number of very large and organizationally complex districts currently have superintendents with relatively few years of service in the superintendency." According to the authors, in a study by the Council of Great City Schools the mean tenure rate was 3.1 years.

Superintendent turnover is continuous and inevitable too. *USA Today* (2008) reports in an article headlined "Urban School Superintendents Hard to Keep," that although urban superintendent's salaries and perks are good, the average urban superintendent nationwide remains in his or her position for less than five years. And specifically since 2003, St. Louis is looking for its eighth superintendent and Kansas City in the last thirty-nine years is on its twenty-fifth superintendent.

It is clear there is a high turnover rate in teacher, principal, and superintendent positions. However, to be fair, some school leader position change is to be expected because of personal choice and normal career ladders. Although change can be healthy, too much change, or a "passing presence" (Brayman & Frink, 2006), is not healthy for any school system. Sustained school reform takes time and requires a leader who is willing to stay the course and develop trusting professional relationships. It also requires the system to treat the leader fairly. This chapter contains tips and suggestions in assisting you to retain your job, become less transient and enjoy your life's work.

Acknowledge When You Have Made a Mistake.

Judges and umpires are not right all the time, nor are school leaders, but failing to admit your mistakes, apologize sincerely, and fix the mistake maximizes the impression this act can have on others in the school organization. We have all seen the impact big and small mistakes have when they have been investigated and improper communication, poor decision making, and inappropriate action have taken place. We don't have to go far to see improprieties or former misuse of power in office. Just look at U.S. presidents or state governors for starters.

A prominent corporation trains its employees to apologize to guests even when they are not wrong so that a positive attitude and impression remains. So why is this act of apologizing so important that school leaders should consider it as well? An apology is a way to lead by example, demonstrating what is important in the organization so that when followers make a mistake they have a role model to consider. Another reason to apologize is because it takes the "wind out of a person's sail." By this I mean sometimes all that a person wants is an apology and the accompanying apologetic words so that the person may consider the case closed. At the least, people know you are concerned. By seizing this opportunity, a school leader can take a negative experience like making a mistake and change it into a positive one for all involved. Generally speaking, people are waiting to see what you are going to do and what is going to happen next.

Unfortunately, all too often, mistakes are made and nothing happens. Others are blamed for the blunder or mistruths are blamed on ambiguous entities such as, "It is the central office's fault;" "There is no money left in the budget;" or even better yet, "The parents are the ones!" Sometimes excuses are made for minor errors such as, "I got so busy, I forgot" or "I lost track of time." Even worse, leaders say they were misquoted and didn't say what others have come to know as the truth, leaving followers to question the leader's credibility.

What are steps that a school leader could follow when mistakes are made? Here are some suggestions:

1. Admit the mistake and apologize for it.
2. Determine exactly what happened so you can correct it. Consider this phrase: "If I had to do it over again I would...."
3. Wherever possible fix the mistake immediately by remedying it and reducing the chance that it will be repeated.

Whether it's an error in scheduling or not calling a snow day during a blizzard, school leaders must take responsibility for their mistakes, accept ownership, set a positive example, and work toward positive solutions. Many times, colleagues and stakeholders just want to hear, "I was wrong and I apologize."

Act as If Each Day Were Your Last.

Approximately two years ago, George Steffen, superintendent of Trevor-Wilmot Consolidated School District in Wisconsin, suffered a major heart attack while at work and his staff came to his rescue. They had been trained in the use of a defibrillator and CPR. As a result they saved his life.

With respect to the staff saving their superintendent, Kathleen Trohler, a reporter for *The Kenosha News*, reported in her front page article (March 24, 2007), "'If not for them we would have arrived and found a pulseless, not breathing male on the ground. We would have found a dead body,' said Pam Oldenburg, a Salem Fire and Rescue Department paramedic and an emergency medical services instructor."

George, who is a bright and witty gentleman, shared with me that "I told Pam she should have said the following to the *Kenosha News*: 'If not for them I would have found a handsome, good-looking male in peak condition resting on the floor.'" This line is so typical of the fifty-eight-year-old Steffen who has dedicated his career to children, works extremely hard, and cares deeply about life, family, and doing the right thing. He epitomizes a moral educator committed to the doing the best for our profession. "Every day counts. Make a difference."

Unfortunately, we will all have a last day, whether it is in our classroom, our office, or better yet at a ripe old age enjoying retirement in the sun and reading a book. The question is whether we have George's sense of humor, compassion, and ability to understand that life is precious. George has had multiple jobs as a teacher and school administrator. He knows that when one door closes another one opens. He is an eternal optimist and a cherished friend.

Despite George's heart attack and previous battle with cancer, he continues to work hard everyday. As a superintendent, he makes every day count. He also knows he is a strong and capable, yet humble leader who could lead in a multitude of environments. We all face rejection at some point in our lives. In the end, however, the key is to realize that your confidence in yourself and your commitment to children are the qualities that will sustain you—wherever you are. So pray you will never need your colleagues to save your And perhaps pray even harder that you are doing the right things so that they will want to save you.

Be Lavish in Your Praise and Miserly in Your Criticism.

Smart school leaders know there is power in praise. It's not the kind of power that is manipulative and underhanded, but the kind of power that is relinquished to help individuals be the best professionals they can be. "Genuine praise" from school leaders lets colleagues (and students, too) know that they are on the right track, realize you are generally happy with their work and meeting your expectations. "Genuine praise" can build a teacher's confidence, give the teacher license to try something new, continue with a technique or strategy that is difficult, and help the person grow and develop toward becoming a more effective professional. This is powerful.

Some of my graduate students, who are full-time teachers, tell me that they can go through the entire school year without having anyone supervise them formally, provide them with feedback on their teaching, or praise them on any aspect of their work. This is crushing to hear.

"Genuine praise" is very different than (what I will call) "praise for the sake of praise." "Genuine praise" is worthy of your time and attention and the activity observed. If you are repeatedly saying "good job," then I would guess you are misusing those words or working with pets. "Genuine praise" should be specific rather than general so the receiver knows exactly what is going right, such as "Were you aware of how many students were engaged in thought with that well-designed question you asked?" Additionally "genuine praise" is immediate rather than delayed, so that the experience is shared between individuals and does not lose meaning over time. Another aspect of "genuine praise" is to remember to tell people how you feel, pinpointing the praise for the receiver. For example, "I was almost moved to tears by the story you told at the assembly. You were awesome!"

Then there is criticism. When individuals receiving the negative comments already feel accepted, the relationship between the giver and receiver of criticism is solid and there is desire and hope of making change, constructive criticism with diplomacy and without emotion can have very positive results. Constructive criticism should focus on the unwanted behavior, not the person. For example a teacher with classroom management issues doesn't need to hear an emotionally laden statement such as, "Your whole class is out of control! What are you going to do about it?" What the teacher does need is emotional and professional support and constructive suggestions to work through the problem. All too often criticism is delivered poorly and the working relationship is permanently damaged.

In most cases, finding the right balance between praise and criticism is delicate. Some say it is 10:1 or 4:1—meaning for every ten or four positive praise comments you can introduce a constructive criticism. But who is really counting each occurrence? Don't lose ground with your delivery of "genuine praise" and constructive criticism. Watch your style of delivery and your approach with people. Remember that sarcasm and indifference delivers the wrong critical message. Be lavish with your "genuine praise" and misery in criticism. If time permits take the time to rehearse your message and think about how it is going to be received. Each and every word counts.

Become Teflon.

The Dupont Company has the trademark on the product Teflon. Most of us will know this product from their nonstick frying pans. It is also used with products such as fabrics for stain protection, wiper blades to reduce friction and extend life, car wax for surface protection from the elements, racing sailboats for smoothness, lens coating for eyeglasses, and even for cables in the telecommunications industry. Wow, that's a lot of uses for a product that just gets "things" not to stick. Have you ever wondered how they get Teflon to stick to the pan?

Being like Teflon surely has its benefits in our profession. As educational leaders we seem to be like electromagnets when it comes to problems. They just have a way of attracting themselves to us. For a variety of reasons, problems have a way of making their way to our door. It may be because we have a sympathetic ear. It may be because we are the classroom teacher. It may be because we are the school administrator and the last recourse. It usually isn't because we were in the wrong place at the wrong time.

The key to problems is getting them solved and not having their remnants stick to you. It's like the movie *Ghostbusters* when a ghostbuster uses a proton pack and destroys a ghost. You don't want to look like a bystander with ectoplasm all over you. When we do solve or help to solve a problem, we occasionally get kudos from our audience and probably feel pretty good about it. There are some problems, however, that we as individuals will not solve. Problems such as those associated with extreme poverty and violence. We are not expected as individuals to solve those problems by ourselves. But there are a multitude of problems that come our way that we try to solve but not to everybody's liking and, on occasion, to no one's liking—such as searching for extra classroom space, suspending a student, trying to pass a referendum, or redrawing district attendance boundary lines. Sometimes we just get dealt a really bad hand. So what do you do? How do you get by, look smart, retain your respect, and not lose your job? You do it by becoming Teflon. You become that nonstick surface that repels the remnants of ill feelings.

Here are some Teflon tips to become nonstick.

1. Put the children in your first sentence then throughout the conversation; for example, "Our children need smaller class sizes in this proposal." "Mary is a charming and a wonderful student in class, but she did pull that chair out from underneath her friend."
2. When possible use consultants or people outside the immediate school system to shoulder potential blame; for example, "Our demographer produced those numbers." "Our architect developed the budget for that project." "The auditor reviewed those accounts." "The language arts consultant helped us with that curriculum."
3. Form committees and heed their advice. Put the naysayers on the committees. It will keep them busy. They can have the success but have to take some responsibility for the problems. Just be willing to put up with the extended conversations, a small price to pay for continued success.
4. Listen and give people your time because sometimes that is all they need.
5. Be consistently positive, especially in the down times.
6. Decide if this is a problem worth battling over; if yes, state upfront that you are responsible and working on it. Take the lead. "I am responsible" goes a long way.
7. Go the extra mile for everyone and as often as you can.
8. Stay with problems. They linger, outlast, out talk, out think, and out plan any one who comes your way.

9. Be honest, open, and have a dialogue about problems, but when the situation calls for discretion, be professional. You might say, "Sorry I can't talk about this but I really wish I could."
10. Show the right emotion for the right situation. If you are the principal on the local news interviewed about an employee accused of giving students alcohol on a field trip, you better look concerned, upset, sad, and talk about what will be done right for the children.
11. If possible, state what you will do differently in the future to prevent a recurrence of the problem.
12. Most importantly show you care for children everyday. They will be your greatest source of power and public relations. They carry the most weight (and should!). They will tell their parents and others you care. They are an army of ambassadors and will be there for you.

So for longevity, spray coat yourself with a little Teflon and hope it sticks.

Being Right Is Overrated.

My first lesson in "being right" came from raising two teenagers. Any one who has been a parent quickly learns that adolescents seem to know it all and are quick to tell you that you know very little to nothing. They resist, become antagonistic and aggressive, and have difficulty accepting another viewpoint. As my former teenagers would tell me, "Mom, you live in the 80s." This attitude, for the most part, is a normal growing up process for teenagers as they mature into young adults. They soon realize there are a few things they really do not know, that naturally you do know, and begin to mellow and soften.

My second lesson in "being right" came from observing a fellow colleague. His style of leadership was authoritarian to say the least. There was only one way to enter a school building, pass a referendum, solve a problem, have graduation, hire a teacher, or prepare for an institute day. His school had the "right" textbook for math (or for any class for that matter) and the teachers in his school knew exactly the "right way" to teach the book. It was clear to all employees in his world that it was "his way or the highway." In fact, when he was tired of listening to opposing opinions he would say, "dismissed" and ask individuals to leave his office. One could even say there was a sense of fear about his "being right" leadership style. As I reflect on this type of attitude and style, I can see an ego that could not afford to be wrong.

His attitude was a venue for showing off, paternally knowing what is best for everyone and giving an impression of "knowing it all." Just like some teenager, his style was combative, confrontational, and challenging.

It is delusional to think there is only one way to approach problems in a school—the leader's way. The reality of school leadership is that it is fast paced, complex, and needing compromise, acceptance, and collegiality. The school leader should become a filter through which all ideas are considered and then a facilitator in order to extract thoughts toward quality decisions.

Don't become a "being right addict"—one who is observed and perceived through word and body language as narrow-minded and intolerant of allowing for an open flow of ideas. It is easy to come away from a meeting with a sense of "I am so glad everyone saw it my way." When one insists on "being right" (and you know I am right about this!), there is a strong possibility of patronage by adults who do not want to cause waves, especially if the individual is their immediate supervisor. A habitual pattern of being right can be perceived by teachers as, "Why are we going through this, when you know it is going to be her way in the end?" By honestly opening one's mind to other possibilities, a school leader will experience the luxury and beauty of learning from others.

Break Bread.

As a teacher I was a little jealous of the three-martini lunch. I pictured a couple of businessmen in their expensive suits and ties chewing the fat, sipping on their drinks, and enjoying a steak luncheon, all at the taxpayers' expense. I felt that way in 1978 when I left the classroom after six years of teaching to join the marketing staff at *Instructor Magazine.* My thoughts on high-rolling fat-cats quickly changed to advertising quotas, the competition, monthly closings, and "at-will" employment. Granted there were some wonderful lunches, and dinners, too, for that matter, with owners of companies and executives of publishing corporations, but there was always one purpose in mind—business. One rarely lost sight of the goal—a business transaction. I had the unique opportunity to learn the education field from the other side, even helped draw an ad for a startup company, Carson-Dellosa, and watch them grow into an incredibly successful business. The "real world" of business is not too much different from our "real world" of schooling. They are both awfully tough places. There is certainly a lot of pressure to succeed in both of them. The business world was like having the *No Child Left Behind Act* looking over your shoulder everyday.

Needless to say, working for a major educational publication was a real eye-opener for a person with no formal business or travel experience. Being gone nearly every other week was not fun. Airport lines and hotels got old very quickly. But I learned so much. My mentor taught me about marketing, sales, and the value of persistency, humor, goodwill, empathy, articulate and exacting speech, and even how to dress. Yes, even how to dress! I remember him telling me to always wear a nice suit and tie and specifically one that, after you left your client's office, no one would remember. You want them to remember what you said, and, yes indeed, you were dressed well.

One of the most important things I learned working for *Instructor Magazine* was the value of breaking bread. Sitting down and talking with people in a dining situation really provides you with an opportunity to learn boatloads about that other person. You become closer, more empathetic, understand each other better, and usually end up with an advocate. And that helps you to solve problems faster based on more intimate personal knowledge, enhances honesty in relationships, and improves familiarity with family. In business it usually amounts to increased business. Your call or email usually gets returned faster, and your ability to conduct business is exponentially enhanced. Most conversations in schools, lunchtime or otherwise, tend to revolve around schools and the children. When breaking bread it can be very interesting, even uncanny, at how much everyone has in common.

Unfortunately, the scheduling dynamics of our profession do not usually allow us much time to have a relaxing lunch. We are usually squeezing in a thirty-minute lunch, perhaps in the teachers' lounge, while a student is knocking on the door or a colleague has an important question to ask. On occasion we have the "Thank God it's Friday" (TGIF) gathering, which brings people together, but usually at a time when everyone is laughing loudly because they are so exhausted from the week. By Friday I was usually spent, and just hoping for a little time to recharge my batteries.

All teachers and administrators should take time off for a relaxed lunch once in a while. When I was principal a few of my teachers would religiously go for lunch once a week. They had to sign out for attendance reasons in case of a fire or lockdown drill. But they came back stronger as a team for having done so. I do understand how challenging it is to get away, but make an attempt to do so. Or have breakfast together. At a minimum make an attempt to do it with the people you work the closest with. Weaknesses have a way of becoming self-evident. Breaking bread helps one to look beyond people's weaknesses to their inner self and strengths and their willingness to help. It provides you with in-depth knowledge of their abilities to be successful contributors to the school environment. And the learning is mutual.

Can't Please People All of the Time, But You Certainly Can Try.

I remember meeting with Mrs. ____, who virtually always had suggestions for program improvement coupled with criticisms of my leadership. I would listen carefully, be polite and courteous, and try to ferret out which aspects of her concerns were valid and which were not. Which ones, if any, I could be a catalyst for doing something about. She, being a chronic complainer, made it difficult, even for me, to put my best foot forward and listen carefully, intently, and with all due diligence. I remember one year a concern was presented on the last day of school. Anyone who works in schools knows what the last day of school is like. Needless to say, last days are usually very interesting ones, filled with mixed emotions and a plethora of details for all school employees to deal with. Mrs. ____ had arrived for a chat about yet another concern. After we finished our discussion, which I did keep brief, it being the last day of school and all, I said, "You know Mrs. ____, I really am working *very* hard to try and please you. I really am working hard to resolve your concerns as best I can." She simply looked at me in the eyes and with a somber voice said, "Well, Howard, it looks like you are just going to have to work harder." I remember smiling and stating something like have a great summer and don't forget I will be here all summer if you need me. I was really thinking "I hope she takes a long vacation."

You know it is really hard, if not nearly impossible, to please everyone all the time. Many people would ask, why even try? Why waste your time? Who cares anyway? Just do your job and move on. Although that attitude may work for some, it has been my personal goal and pleasure to try to please everyone. I try to find that kernel of truth in the person's concern that I may be able to be address. I actually take complaints on as a personal challenge—sort of the Olympic Complaining Competition. I felt like I would either win the Gold, Silver, or Bronze depending on how well the concerned parent felt after he or she left. Several times I won no medal at all. But the point here is that other than a little lost time, and rather than *lost* I prefer to use the word *invested*, there is no harm in making an honest attempt to try and please (or problem solve) for someone. At the end of the day you may be tired, may or may not have a few Olympic medals, but for certain you will have tried your best and be viewed positively by the community as a whole for treating the person with dignity and respect. Some community members even felt a little sorry for me when they would see who was complaining. Life brings you lemons; you can drive them, squeeze them, or grumble about them. Best to remain positive and just try and make some lemonade and smile. If you see *those* people coming, don't duck, don't run, and don't hide. View them as a challenge, go for the Gold, settle for Silver or Bronze, and move on to your next problem. You will be happier and healthier for having given it your best shot and for not having taken anything personally. Save your high stress level for the serious things in life—for example, for the child, parent, colleague, or friend who has a serious illness.

And yes, as summer turned to fall, I did try harder the following year with Mrs. ____. Honestly, it really didn't matter much and she never really did change her disposition. But for those who saw the way I acted toward her, it did matter. And, in many ways, I did feel good about giving it my best shot.

Come Early, Stay Late, and Don't Do Your Income Tax at Work.

We designed and presented a workshop entitled "Student Teaching Tips from the Principal's Perspective" to prospective student teachers ready to embark on their first student teaching experience. In our presentation, we stressed the importance of coming early to work, staying late, and seeking opportunities to assist the school in any way possible, because in essence the novice teacher is always being evaluated, interviewed if you will, every minute they are present at school. This appraisal starts the second one walks through the door in the morning, continues throughout the day, and concludes when one leaves from the school at night. Additionally, if this school is a potential place where one might want to find permanent employment as a teacher, observations and informal interviews are occurring all the time by all stakeholders.

The aforementioned discussion also applies to school leaders. Your work of leading is being evaluated, observed, and critically assessed every moment you are on the job. Do you spend too much time in your office alone on personal matters such as dreaded income tax returns or reviewing online your personal investment portfolio while the business of educating children unfolds without you? Do you say to yourself, "Well, I'm here. Isn't that enough?"

Certainly there is a broad range when thinking about a leader's work ethic. There are slackers to workaholics. Every smart school district wants a leader who has a strong work ethic and on occasion you will see this characteristic listed in a job vacancy notice. After all who wants a leader with a mere satisfactory work ethic or one who could be characterized as "doing the minimum." Schools need leaders who are reliable, ambitious, intuitive, and get things done. These leaders seek out opportunities to do more than their job descriptions state. They do the work now, do it right, stay on task, and focus on results. This persistence defines the leader's work ethic as one who has a set of values and habits based on hard work and discipline. So keep your nose to the grindstone and consider hiring a tax accountant.

Deal with the Data Flood.

School districts generate large quantities of data, charts, and graphs—electronic warehouses waiting to be tapped and analyzed. There are personnel inventories, school enrollment statistics, class size figures, student records, budget information, monthly attendance reports, graduation and dropout rates, parent visitation percentages, and test results, just to name a few. Schools must store, analyze, interpret, and report data regularly to a variety of audiences as a result of the current accountability trend and effect of the government initiative in *No Child Left Behind* (NCLB). With the deluge of daily school data, leaders face extraordinary challenges in the use of data. Here are six recommendations to consider:

1. Develop a culture of inquiry. Make working with data as common and normal as filling out a requisition form. Educators should not view it as an "add-on" by already overwhelmed professionals, but a way to welcome the opportunity to examine ways to become more effective.
2. Manage the constant flow of data that you are dealing with. Sort, filter, and figure out what data meets your purpose. Check its quality, sources, and formats so that the data is at the point that you (and others) can work with it. Take the lead on this.
3. Provide sufficient time to support data conversations. Professional development opportunities are one of the best venues for these rich dialogues. Build them into your professional development plans.
4. Reduce blaming and finger pointing. I remember conversations that went something like this: "If only the English teachers would have taught this we wouldn't have _____ *(you fill in)* today." Squelch this conversation and direct the discussion toward what needs to be done now.
5. Build school personnel data analysis and interpretation skills. Working alone with data can be deadly. Support a team ap-

proach. What do *we* want to know? How effective is *our* new math program or intervention? What trends do *we* see in the data?

6. Pay attention to the audience that is receiving the information. Use the data wisely, appropriately, and ethically.

The primary goal of data is to inform and improve instruction. To make sense of the constant flood of information and apply it to the classroom setting requires an instructional leader who can make connections or guide individuals in the right direction. Many leaders, who themselves are uncomfortable with data, may have trouble convincing others of their ideas or plans. Without data to back up a plan or proposal, it is hard for anyone to believe that new innovations, strategies, or changes might work. Leaders who deal with data productively and effectively feel like they have control over their fate and the future of their classroom, department, or school. This feeling accompanies a desire to know more, know why, and know what might come next?

Don't Be a Product of Buzzword Bingo.

Two teachers in my graduate class, Jen and Min, started giggling and talking about a game they played during faculty meetings at their school called *Buzzword Bingo*. It appears that their principal did not facilitate inspiring and thought-provoking meetings and most faculty at their school had to resort to other means to keep themselves attentive and alert. Prior to a faculty meeting, Bingo cards would circulate on email and faculty members would print out a card for the meeting. The traditional five-by-five grid would hold predictable words and short phrases that the leader would say and each faculty member would put an "X" through the word said by the leader at the meeting. To keep the game secretive and keep their jobs, faculty members who got Bingo would not shout out "Bingo," but would wait until after the meeting to settle up with their colleagues.

While I have never observed one of these school Bingo cards, I was surprised that *Buzzword Bingo* has many entries on the Internet. One site in particular, www.meetingbingo.net, has several *Meeting Bingo* cards that one can print out, as well as references to *Business Buzzword Bingo*. Of concern is why aren't colleagues involved or engaged in professional meetings?

Let's think about ways to stamp out *Buzzword Bingo*. Replace the groans of an announcement of a meeting with eager educators gathering to share professional issues and conduct an effective and productive meeting. Here are some ideas to check:

What is the purpose of the meeting? Is it to make decisions; dispense information; express concerns; problem solve; evaluate progress toward goals; plan; celebrate successes; determine new procedures; and/or get feedback? Is there a better alternative than having this meeting in order to respect everyone's time? Can I cancel the meeting and use another communication source such as email or a memo?

What should be on the agenda? In advance ask for input from those coming to the meeting as well as to your items, and provide the agenda approximately a week prior to the meeting.

How much time should be spent on each agenda item? Label each item as to what kind of input is expected from the meeting participants, how much time is allocated to the item, and who will be presenting the information. For example: Item #6 Technology update…Mary Smit…no action—presentation of new materials 3:00–3:30 pm.

When should the meeting start and end? Start and end each meeting on time. Try to set the meeting dates for the whole year so that individuals know in advance the date and time of each meeting and can plan ahead. Choosing the same day of the week, when possible, helps people to remember the meeting date; for example, meeting the second Tuesday of every month becomes easier to remember. This action shows respect for the meeting and those who are attending.

How did the meeting go? The leader of the meeting should evaluate the event as to feedback and/or suggestions by the group and what was accomplished so that the next meeting will be even better.

Faculty and staff who are spending their time designing Bingo cards in anticipation of a dreaded meeting are not seeing this time as meaningful and important. It also illustrates a lack of confidence in the leader and a culture of disrespect. Although faculty and staff cannot be coaxed into becoming a professional learning community, this concept can be cultivated over time through productive meetings. A faculty meeting is the perfect time to demonstrate an environment that nurtures and supports professionals by first using their time properly. So don't be a product of *Buzzword Bingo* (see sample card below).

School Leader Buzzword Bingo

B	I	N	G	O
Benchmarks	IEP	NCLB	Global Learner	Outcomes-based
Best Practice	Information Highway	Network	Goal Setting	One-Size-Fits All
Block Scheduling	Identifying Highly Qualified Teachers	Free Space	Gifted Students	Our Mission
Board of Education	Improvement Plan	Norm Reference Tests	Gender Equity	Out-of-the-Box
Big Picture	Involving Parents	Needs of ELL, ESL	Grade/Dept.-Level Meetings	Offering Character Education

Expect the Ripple Effect.

Growing up in the 1950s in Chicago was a delightful and adventurous experience. Minimal finances made sandlot baseball, tackle football without equipment, and collecting empty pop bottles for the two-cent return regular occurrences. Summers, amidst gainful employment, consisted of long walks to North Avenue beach where my friends and I dove off a portion of the Lake Michigan pier to find whole clay pigeons resting on the lake's floor. Whole or in part clay pigeons were remnants from the nearby skeet shooting range. On occasion we would skim rocks along the lake to see who could skim the furthest. We would search for the flattest rock and throw it parallel to the water to see how many times it would bounce off the water. The person with the most bounces was the winner. One couldn't help but notice the constant ripple effect the skimmed rock had on the water. I was astounded to find that there is a website with a rock skimming champ video: http://www.stupidity.com/play-9542-Rock-Skimming-Champion.html. In spite of the title *stupidity.com*, this video is worth a thousand words. Just watch that rock skim and its subsequent rippling effect on the water. School leader decisions can be just like that rock skimming the surface of the water.

Sir Isaac Newton's third law of physics states that every action has an equal and opposite reaction. Well, I have concluded that many school leader actions can have unequal, opposing, unintended, and even hidden reactions or, perhaps better worded, consequences, just like the rock skimming over the water.

Think about these situations:

A teacher chooses to highly compliment or painfully criticize a child in class. By the end of the day, parents, relatives, extended relatives, the child's friends and their parents, and the community at-large, and even the faculty might all be calling the school leader. We know that a teacher's words can inspire or extinguish a student's dreams. They can also start a chain of events that appear to be never ending.

A school principal witnesses thieves stealing several students' bicycles and decides to confront the thieves by himself. He chases after them but, alas, they escape. Local law enforcement reprimands him because he didn't notify them first, and some community members question his common sense. The local press ultimately wrote the following headline, "School Chief Gives Chase," and concludes the article with a quote stating something like, "I just get upset when they steal *my* students' bicycles." Everyone was talking about this by the end of the day. He learned quickly not to try and be a hero. (OK, I did this in the 1980s.)

A school superintendent, who even for the best of reasons, releases a classroom teacher for incompetence. The teacher's personal and family life is turned completely upside down, as well as the teacher's classroom, colleagues, and community in which the teacher serves. I remember thinking about the ripple effect the first time I released a teacher. I realized the effect but knew the dismissal was the right thing to do. Point being, do the right thing but understand the consequences of your actions and decisions.

Ripples can be good and ripples can be bad. A wise person once said to hope for the best and plan for the worst. Positive ripples usually don't need to be planned for, but the intended and unintended consequences of the negative ripples must be taken into account, carefully analyzed, and seriously planned for.

Find Challenges Before Someone Finds Them for You.

How many parents have strolled into your classroom and said, "My child is not challenged"? How many parents have walked into your administrative office and said, "Our school could be so much better if only you would just..."? How many board members, during a meeting, have raised their hand and said, "I've been hearing that our children are having difficulty with..."?

In our profession there is never (I normally caution against the use of the words *always* and *never*, but *never* is the right choice here) a time when demands are not placed on us. Rare is the time when we even have a minute to breathe—let alone a time when we are not challenged. Have you ever heard, "Boy, she has nothing to do"? Having a lot to do is great. But one just has to have the right things to do and be focused in the right direction because challenges are our friends.

Just getting through the day is not good enough.

Just managing the daily barrage of events is not good enough.

Just being efficient is not good enough.

Just being polite, courteous, and kind is not good enough.

"Just" doesn't cut it.

You have to have challenges—real challenges and I mean the time-consuming ones. You have to get better; you have to want to get better; you have to have goals; you have to wake up saying, "Yeah, I hope today goes fine and there are no major problems to deal with but at the end of this day, at the end of this week, at the end of this year, my teaching will be better; I will be a better principal; I will be smarter, sharper,...and, in short, things will be better today than yesterday for children." You have to just want to get a little better every day—incremental improvement.

We know the value of strategic planning and long- and short-term goals and objectives—they provide a blueprint for betterment. If you don't have goals, if you don't have everybody busy getting better, then *they* will figure out what *you* should be doing to get better. Many will suggest improvement ideas anyway, but at least if you have enough to do, enough to work on, they may stay out of your way. At a minimum you will have a litany of items that you can say are in progress. As a teacher I had goals for each of my students. As a principal I had goals for my building, my staff, and myself. As a business manager I had goals for the improvement and integrity of our financial reporting. As a superintendent I had pages and pages of long- and short-term goals and objectives, developed with the assistance of the staff, board, community surveys, etc., and approved by the board, which were reported on quarterly as being in progress, partially completed, or completed. Everyone had a role to play in their success. Why? Because if I didn't then every Tom, Dick, and Mary who wants something done because of their pet peeve would march in and tell me to do this or that. When you are busy—busy doing the right stuff and being future focused—it provides a shield for you to say "no." The problems and suggestions will still be posited, but you will be able to say "sorry, not now."

For example many of us review and update our curriculum on a curriculum-renewal cycle. If someone was complaining about my math program, stating the program focuses too much on application and analysis at the expense of basic math computation skills, I would say, "I hear what you are saying, but that program is not up for review for two more years. I am noting your concern, please ask your child's teacher to share some things you can do at home, and I will be sure your concern is brought up during our next review." If someone didn't like our program, they just had to wait. As an aside my district's assistant superintendent introduced semiannual CAP (curriculum articulation and planning) meetings. These meetings were a time for teachers to meet and discuss minor changes to a program. The purpose of CAP meetings was so that when we began a review according to the cycle, the staff wasn't shocked to find that the whole program had changed over the years in between a review.

Wanting to be busy, being busy, keeping busy, working on the right stuff, with roadmaps and blueprints for improvement, helps to minimize a sense of urgency, reflects a strong intellect, and assists in reducing the number of "me first" people who will come your way every day. At a minimum, finding challenges will provide you with ammunition in your attempt to have them steer clear. Over the years several of my board members have said to me, "Howard you didn't get everything done as fast as I wanted, but, in due time, everything did get addressed. I just wish my children were starting school now instead of graduating."

Grow to Be a Change Agent or Change Your Address.

Change is everywhere—constant and continuous, big and small, serious and inconsequential. Change can affect us personally and directly such as when a new student joins a class or an administrator has to recommend to the board to reduce personnel. There is institutional change, such as hiring a new principal, designing policies for student safety, or closing a school. Then there is societal change, like electing a new president, implementing federal and state mandates, staying up-to-date on special education law, and college admission requirements. Change can be massive, ambiguous, unpredictable, complex, and deeply intertwined.

One superintendent I worked for was nicknamed the "moving superintendent." As a result of large subdivisions being rapidly built in the community and a couple of hundred children moving into new homes every year, it was very difficult to plan for the exploding student population. During the building boom one spring, the "moving superintendent" announced that because the children were being moved around the school district to make classroom size more equitable per the teacher contract, all eight principals would be moving to a different building in the fall. With shocked faces, the questions began from the principals. Can I bring my secretary? No. Can I bring my custodians? No. Can I bring some teachers? Finally, a yes, but only if they choose to move, there are openings in the school, and the sending and receiving principals agree. And so it happened, massive, mandatory, disruptive, complicated, and significant change.

Some leaders may choose to be quick-change artists—those who enjoy change for the sake of change. These leaders dwell on the bits and pieces of change, such as thinking about new ways to get parents involved in school at the expense of missing the real value of actually getting them there. Strewn around them are fragmented attempts at change, but nothing really changes notably. Some school leaders keep adding things for teachers to do, such as implementing new instructional strategies, reviewing technology software, readjusting attendance policies on the spot, but not clarifying either what is to be removed that may not be working or is the value added. Teachers become overloaded, confused, agitated, and ultimately return to what is comfortable—the status quo. Pity the educators who have a school leader who goes to a conference and *immediately* tries to implement the newest curriculum trend, like block scheduling, just to keep up with a neighboring school. Change doesn't happen magically because you want it to or say so. Nor do you have to be The Great Houdini to make it happen.

Boards of education, local school councils, trustees, and governing bodies want school leaders who can grow in the journey toward change with their faculty and staff and get results together. Leaders who facilitate teachers to be agents of change, enablers of change, reduce them as casualties of change.

Certainly a school leader does not make change happen alone. But how do you get other educators to "buy-in" and/or take ownership of change? It is not a good idea to use the Nike slogan, *Just Do It*. Nor in this case would

I suggest following the advice of Sheryl Crow in her classic song, *Change Will Do You Good*. Most educators I know will not accept change without a variety of opportunities to interact and collaborate with colleagues about it. Change leaders need to grow in their facilitation skills so that they can challenge educators to independently, collaboratively, and creatively search for the best possible ideas to put in practice. Additionally, this type of leader has the insight to know what is important locally and focuses on the things that will make a difference in the school for students. But this is just the beginning.

So that you don't have the " innovation, strategy, or policy flavor of the month," know that real change can only occur when it is sustained over time. Only then will educators and stakeholders know the change is important and that it reflects the best we know about teaching and learning. If you are not willing to integrate and support change throughout the system, it may be time to change your address, go into hiding, and/or put another person in charge. All aspects of the system need to be moving forward together. A dentist doesn't say, "Well I guess I won't worry about that abscessed tooth, the rest of your mouth is fine." The school systems and individuals in the schools are interdependent for support and each person contributes to successful, substantive and sustained change.

Leverage Technology to Your Advantage.

It was 1985 and I had been superintendent for a couple years. Being a small school district, I was responsible for the levy. A critical but daunting task of determining the financial needs of the school district on a fund-by-fund basis and translating those needs into the amount requested in taxes. I remember spending about 40 hours just trying to apply a complicated set of mathematical formulas, some of which I had created, using paper, pencil, and a calculator. The task was critical and there was little room for error. One day a school board member introduced me to *VisiCalc*—the first spreadsheet program. We spent an entire morning entering the formulas in the computer and, subsequently, the levy data for that year. It was nearly lunchtime when I pressed the final key. I couldn't believe it. The levy numbers just popped up on the screen. I hit print and was done. From that time on I only needed to enter the yearly data and the calculations magically appeared. It was then and there that I learned the power of technology and the need to leverage that power to maximize efficiency and eliminate redundancies to survive the demands of a job that is never ending.

More than two decades have passed since I was introduced to *VisiCalc*. I now liken technology, specifically my laptop, to my wallet. As my wallet contains the critical documents for identification and purchasing, my laptop contains the viable information for me to do my job—parts of which can be done from anywhere in the world. Although the computer will not replace the critical face-to-face interaction with students, colleagues, and staff, it will enable you to do most anything at any time. My laptop is joined to my hip as much as my wallet is in my back pocket. Just consider the following school leader responsibilities that can be accomplished almost anywhere and at almost anytime on a laptop:

- Communicating quickly and easily with anyone and everyone as necessary whether individually or in small or large groups.
- Creating *PowerPoint* presentations for your class, faculty, or board meetings.
- Writing employee evaluations or student report cards.
- Being informed of the most up-to-date news from weather reports to matters pertaining to school safety.
- Creating teacher/student schedules, reports, and speeches.
- Taking notes, even minutes of meetings, while in progress and then immediately distributing them.
- Conducting teleconferences and podcasts.

The critical dimension that technology provides is the ability to create and access information immediately in almost anyplace and at anytime, and to communicate that information at a moment's notice. The ubiquitous nature of technology removes many of the barriers I frequently found were at the heart of school problems that could fester over time. At the top of my list were problems created by a real or imagined lack of communication, which was sometimes attributed to lack of caring when, in reality, it was a lack of time to attend to it. Technology provides educational equity by reducing the divide associated with lack of resources and lack of information. Even my phone has become a portable office with built in network connections and a calendar.

Learning to leverage technology is very, very time-consuming. But so is learning CPR (cardiopulmonary resuscitation). In short, it can be a lifesaver.

Navigate the Waters with Barracudas in Mind.

I would say I am pretty pathetic. I don't do much other than work. I don't have any hobbies—don't play golf like many of my friends and colleagues; don't collect coins, stamps, bottles, or postcards like my ever-so-smart bother-in-law, John; don't have that desire to fix up the house—my motto there is "above all else do no harm." I just really enjoy being in schools, being with children. Although *work* does not technically count as a hobby, it has been personally as rewarding as having one. Like I said—pathetic.

About the closest I have ever come to a hobby was having a seventy-five-gallon saltwater reef tank. A former student (nice to have those former students around), and current operator of a saltwater aquarium company, maintained it for me. The children always loved to feed the fish or check out their beautiful colors. The corals were also striking and ever so intriguing. Watching a starfish triple in size or a banded coral shrimp dance on a rock can be quite amusing and, of course, educational. The children called it the *Finding Nemo* tank because of all the similarities to the Disney movie. The tank kept them coming back to experience my "field trip" office. There was always something fascinating happening in that tank. Late night work or meetings were more relaxed with the overhead moon light that glimmered over the top of the tank. Most importantly I learned a lot about a coral reef aquarium. I learned the importance of compatibility and the critical balance that exists from salinity and pH levels to lighting and making sure that aggressive fish or deadly corals were not part of the mix. Just one incompatible fish or one wrong coral had the potential to be catastrophic. It reminded me of the balance that exists in schools and, for that matter, in life.

Ever since having a freshwater aquarium in my first fifth grade classroom, fish have fascinated me. I enjoyed them so much that when I had the opportunity to go scuba diving, I jumped on it. I remember once diving with my son, Nick. We were about thirty-five feet down when off to my right, about ten yards away, was a large barracuda—a ravenous predator that searches out its prey by waiting patiently and surprising its victims with its fast speed and cunning maneuvers. My son took the sighting in stride—perhaps this didn't seem disconcerting being a U.S. Marine with one tour of duty in Iraq under his belt and all. I, on the other hand, was thinking, "Holy __ this is not good!" I remember watching that barracuda float there in suspended animation. I can still see it today. I can still see its teeth. I didn't move. It didn't flinch. A couple minutes went by. It seemed like a lifetime. This large, elongated, predatory fish was definitely getting the best of me. I breathed deeper and deeper from my oxygen tank and then slowly, very slowly, swam away.

In our jobs, there are barracudas waiting for us. Sound like anyone you've met lately? You know those individuals who are lurking in the depths of the school just waiting to do harm. Some will try to discredit you and harm your reputation, whereas others will try to hurt the very mission of your school. Be careful because, like a barracuda, they can swim in schools but also can swim alone. Be vigilant, but not paranoid, about who is lurking around the corner. Keep an eye out for those who would create havoc and do harm. Some people are just down right negative. They thrive on it. Don't get caught off balance. I kept my eyes on that barracuda that day. Never took them off it. Never lost concentration. Waited for the moment to act. Action in that case meant slowly moving away. You should be positive and keep a great sense of humor. But, as a bright person once said, one needs to hope for the best but plan for the worst. Planning includes keeping a close eye out for an attack. Be ever watchful and navigate those waters knowing that there are unfriendlies out there. But know that being alert, aware, ever watchful, and on guard prepares you to deal with whatever predator surfaces.

Purchase Your Back-to-School Survival Supplies.

Every summer, students and their families receive a flood of information about purchasing the necessary school supplies for the upcoming year. In endless newspaper ads, clean-cut sparkling students model the proper attire, backpacks, and supplies representing the proper look and required items for the new school year. Whether students are preparing for kindergarten or high school, the ritual of purchasing school supplies signifies newness, a clean slate, and an opportunity to begin anew. Shouldn't school leaders have that same opportunity? Yes, they should have the same chance to purchase items to renew, refresh, revive, and survive their upcoming school year. What would a survival supply list look like for back to school? Try these items for starters.

1. Aspirin, Tums, No-Doze (no comment needed)
2. Post-it notes and/or small note pads that will fit in your pocket (to remember all those thoughts, requests, and replies during your day)

3. Greeting cards that say *Thank you, Good job, Congratulations* (to immediately respond), and return address labels and stamps
4. Weather alert radio (to plan ahead for bad weather)
5. Unlimited text messaging to others (to communicate with friends, family, and colleagues—if you cannot be with them at least you can text them!)
6. Trinkets for students—candy, awards, pencils, badges, coupons, passes (to acknowledge them)
7. Endless supply of decaf and regular coffee and tea (for you and to be cordial)
8. Current calendar and date book (to be organized)
9. Batteries for radios/walkie-talkies, etc. (to prevent being out of commission)
10. Band-aids and antiseptic (to heal wounds both visible and invisible)
11. Hand sanitizers (to prevent use of sick days)
12. Erasers (to eliminate mistakes)
13. Skin cream (to keep your thick skin normal)
14. Professional journal subscriptions (to be a well-read and knowledgeable leader)
15. Granola/power bars and MREs, a military commodity that provides quick meals ready to eat (to provide access to nourishment when on the go)
16. Poncho/rainwear/umbrella (to dash outside when needed)
17. Change of clothes, shoe polish, toothbrush (to look refreshed for evening meetings)

The opening of a new school year should be an exhilarating and positive experience for everyone, especially the school leader. In some ways, it can become breathtaking and/or leave you breathless because of the high energy needed to make the new year an exciting experience for all. New students, unexpected students and glitches in the system can make a school leader exhausted and headed to the desk drawer for an aspirin. If you are well supplied with the items you need for the new school year and if the students are supplied with their fresh new backpacks, everyone will be well prepared and off to a great start.

Remember That You Have Three Envelopes, But Only Open Two of Them.

On the rare occasion, we do need help when taking a big hit. Although I am a believer in accepting responsibility and blame and being the point person for problems, there are times when reaching out to get assistance in shouldering some of the impact is warranted. Just don't do it more than a couple of times. The following humorous story helps clarify my sentiments.

I really don't know where this story started. If I did I would certainly provide the reference. I have known this story for decades, and, as such, have completely lost sight of its origin. A Google search of "three envelopes" brings up numerous stories, most about CEOs and executives, but the points are similar. I have used this story in speeches and graduate-level classes. In any event here goes.

> A new superintendent was taking the helm of a school district. He bumped into the outgoing superintendent who politely smiled and said he had left him three envelopes in the upper-right-hand desk drawer. They were placed there in case he ran into any significant problems. After the short honeymoon and a year of baptism by fire, the new (now old) superintendent was having some significant labor relations issues. Noting the rising level of grievances and discontent he opened the first envelope. It read: *Blame the former superintendent*. And so he did. He blamed the former superintendent for his lack of follow-through, administrative regulations, and poor past practices. It worked. The concerns went away and life went on.
>
> Two years later parents were complaining about too much teacher academic freedom and the content and lack of curriculum coordination in sex education, creationism versus Darwinism, and choice of library books. Things were getting pretty ugly. Out of desperation the superintendent opened the second envelope. It read: *Form a committee*. And so he did. And to his pleasure it bought him a couple more years of peace. People had their say, consensus was reached, and life went on.
>
> In his fourth year as superintendent, the district was having a referendum. People were mad, as no one wanted their taxes hiked. Fiscal mismanagement was alleged and placed squarely at the hands of the superintendent. Even the referendum ballot was hard

to understand and in question. His support structures had vanished. In a moment of desperation he opened his final envelope. It read: *Write three envelopes.*

When I left the superintendency after twenty-four years, I had planned to leave my replacement three envelopes. But she knew the drill, knew my stories, and would have known the envelopes' contents. Instead, I left her a voodoo doll in a shadow box with extra stickpins. Every now and then I do feel a strong pain in my side! I also know I have it coming. Don't use more than two envelopes during any one stay.

Reserve Your Judgments.

As I was retiring from the superintendency, my wife of thirty-five years was diagnosed with a walnut-sized meningioma brain tumor. What we thought were panic attacks prompted by a Marine son in Iraq, turned out to be seizures. The diagnosis created an immediate strain, concern, and urgency. Absolutely critical was using clear judgment to determine which doctor should perform the surgery. Weighing and evaluating the variables with respect to a very delicate and life-altering surgery was gut wrenching and mind boggling. The right judgment call was paramount and critical. My wife pretty much took it in stride, was extremely positive, and had a very successful operation.

We constantly make judgments every day and many of them are life altering for children and adults. Have you ever thought about all those decisions and judgments you make daily? Have you ever considered the numerous ones that our students make? Think about these.

> What should I wear today?
> How much should I spend?
> What should I eat?
> Should I change jobs?
> What if I do this or that?

Then there are the job-related judgments of:

> Grading papers
> Evaluating teachers
> Conducting parent conferences
> Evaluating curriculum

Implementing classroom management
Responding to children, adults

Then there are those personal judgments being made about *you*. They say you never get a second chance to make a good first impression. Why? Because you are being critiqued. What do people think of me—my clothes, my looks, my character, my attitude, my behavior …? What does my supervisor think of my teaching, my administering? Will I be rehired?

We have a multitude of data points that flash through our brains every day. As we filter them we make judgments about people, places and things. There are parts of our jobs that *require* us to make judgments. As teachers we grade assignments, adjudicate children's disputes, maintain discipline, and discuss and debate the best teaching practices. As administrators we recruit and select employees, evaluate personnel competencies, allocate budgets, and strategically plan for the future.

There are clearly times that our jobs dictate and *require* us to make judgments—to carefully use that gray brain matter and be analytical. But wouldn't life be better if you didn't *have* to? Wouldn't life be a little less stressful if you just listened and didn't feel compelled to make a response—to make a judgment?

The fewer your judgments, the longer your life. Think twice before you judge someone or something. Ask yourself, do I really need to be judgmental? Do I really need to go out on a limb here? Do I have to "weigh in" on this issue? Does my job really demand a judgment on my part? If not, why do it? Some people feel a need to get in the last word or make a qualitative statement in a conversation. Some people believe that their position requires a judgmental response. Not always so.

At a minimum not judging will certainly reduce the "open mouth, insert foot" occasions. So next time you visit a classroom, converse in the teachers' lounge, talk with students in the hallways, or see parents, if the interaction provides you the luxury to do so, just take it all in. Smile and listen. Keep your judgmental thoughts to yourself and reserve those judgments for the times in which they are mandated.

Resist the Resistors.

I don't get it.

This too shall pass.

It's too expensive.

That's not how we do things around here.

We don't have the resources.

Whose idea was this?

I don't trust the people in charge.

What's in it for me?

When am I supposed to do this? I already have enough to do.

This isn't going to work in my class.

What will parents think?

No one asked me my opinion.

It's not my job.

Is it going to be on the state test?

I am not comfortable with this.

The old way is working.

I am not doing it.

I am retiring soon and I don't care.

Maybe you know individuals who say these statements on a regular basis when a new innovation or change is on the horizon. Or possibly, you have said it yourself.

Human beings are creatures of habit, monsters some would say, and enjoy being comfortable; therefore, resisting change comes naturally. Stability and security at times may make our life predictable and calm, but in the world of fast-paced schools, educators rarely have the luxury of "resting on their laurels." If schools were like retail stores, we could close for business, put paper up in the windows, hang a "closed" sign on the door, and reopen when the change was complete. Unfortunately, schools reinvent themselves under the watchful eyes of stakeholders who expect change to take place at the same time school is being conducted. When an educator hears about a new change, the educator may refer to the list of statements above, change the expression on his or her face, dig in his or her heels, and resist.

Some resistors may push you around or bully you with the comments they make. Others may just do nothing and continue to do nothing, daring you to make them change their "do nothing/coasting status." Resistors like to argue the point, challenge you publicly and behind your back, trying to make the change go away so that the peace and calm of the status quo remains. Resistors can gang up on you and make you feel like you are crazy ("But you said…") or by reviewing things over and over ("Now what should we be doing?") or just wear you out by reminding you of past change events that did not go well.

Change leaders translate unpleasant behavior into what resistors are really saying when they refuse. For example, "I am afraid" might mean "I am nontenured and worried about my job." Or "I don't understand" could translate into "I don't think I have the skills or understanding to do this." Or "I am not ready for this change right now" could mean "I am overwhelmed and don't see how I am going to fit this into the expectations you already have for me."

How should you stand firm and protect yourself against the resistors and enact change? First, make sure all the top decision makers are aware and support the change. For example, there is nothing worse than working to implement a curriculum change when a school board decides to abandon it in midstream. Second, explain how the new change will support and connect to the mission and vision of the school. This connection provides a built-in support system when it matches the school's purposes and beliefs. Third, coach educators how the responsibility of the change will reduce their burden over time rather than adding to it. If possible, take a responsibility that has been met "off their plates." Fourth, allow for a risk-free environment that includes continuous and ongoing support. For instance, give teachers opportunities to pilot the change, and to interact and communicate with others on a regular basis, especially those who are experiencing the same innovation. Agree that the change is important, making mistakes is normal, and revisions to the change are acceptable. Fifth, check to make sure everyone has the same vocabulary and is using it appropriately. For instance, is the word *bullying* being defined the same by everyone. Finally, clarify and communicate. By keeping the message of change constant and consistent, followers will understand that the change is not going away. All in all, these strategies reduce the fear of failure, resist the resistors, and optimize the chances for successful change.

Stretch Yourself by Thinking in Alternatives.

While I have very fond memories of my childhood, there were certain events that clearly made some indelible marks on me and defined the ways in which I view and approach problems and problem solving. I frequently think about what I would do if things weren't the way they are or if they should suddenly change. One result of this way of thinking is that when brainstorming solutions to problems, some would say that I am a little "off" or, at a minimum, "off the beaten path," whereas others think I am just creative. I push people to the limits of their creative problem-solving capabilities and then see if their approaches can hold up under great scrutiny. As to being "off," "off the beaten path," or just creative, you be the judge based upon just a few of my childhood stories.

In the 1960s, when my dad's late-model Buick lost its reverse, I thought for sure it was time for him to buy a new car or at least a used one. He drove that car for one year without reverse—a feat that didn't amaze me at the time but sure did as I got older. When I asked him how he could possibly drive without reverse, he commented to me that it is a challenge, but "you just have to plan ahead." As a result, I consistently think about being future focused and seeing problems, and their potential solutions, before they occur.

One time we moved to an apartment on Belmont Avenue, adjacent to a city playground, which my mom and dad didn't think was safe for my sister or me. When I told my dad that the swing set and slide were fun and I needed to go there, he said he would take care of that. The following weekend he bought a playground set and put it in the apartment. Yes, *in* the apartment. I will never forget the loud rocking sound from using the swing set, which wasn't mounted to the ground. In hindsight it was really bizarre and probably partially explains my "different" personality. But as a result, I have consistently inquired about proposed ideas and questioned a presented rationale to detect loopholes, flaws, and knee-jerk reactions.

OK, one more story—In the 1950s and 1960s there wasn't too much worry about legal liability in a friendly neighborhood environment. After a snowstorm my dad would take his car to the nearby church parking lot and tie sleds one by one behind each other and to the car bumper and then drive around the lot in circles. The last sled in the line really got whiplash and would flip and spin around. We usually had five to ten sleds in a line and my friends loved it. As a result I have frequently thought about the thrill of riding that last sled—the hardest one to stay on—the one with the most challenge. Taking the big challenges stretches one's mind and makes one frequently problem solve—the net result is that you get pretty good at it.

In any school on any given day, a very long journey evolves with problems to be solved at every turn. School leaders have a myriad of problems to resolve and frequently need to be diplomatic, flexible and creative in their approach. In short, they all too often have to keep coming up with multiple solutions and put them on the table to see if they work. Be detailed, creative, different, smart, and unique in your thinking. So stretch yourself by thinking in alternatives. It pays off.

My dear father never knew what I really learned from all these adventures. And, unfortunately, he can't now. "Thanks, dad."

5
On Honoring Yourself

Just the thought of honoring yourself is probably disconcerting, challenging, and perhaps even awkward. Inherent in a position of school leadership is frequently the expectation that the school leader will act unselfishly to serve others. In such a helping, guiding, and supportive role, school leaders work diligently facilitating students in their academic achievements and social and emotional development, assisting teachers as they grow and advance in our profession and partnering with parents in their role as guardians.

School leaders may worry that in honoring themselves they might look like they are on an "ego trip"—"It's all about me." A school leader's comments such as, "Look how well our school did on its exams this year!" or "We have made great strides in the last two years under my leadership," may appear to be egotistical and self-serving. The opposite perception might be projected when school leaders do not recognize themselves and appear to be too relaxed, laid back, lack substance, and are too informal. Using the testing example when a school does very well and improves on exams but the leader does not accept credit for any of the success, instead only acknowledging others for "stepping up" and accepting the challenge, may give the impression the leader only credits others or, even worse, allows others to take over the leadership role.

This chapter provides you with ideas to assist you in honoring yourself, accepting that honor, and doing so in the right way—a socially acceptable way. In honoring yourself, we certainly do not mean paying homage to your greatness and your immense self-worth. Most of our parents taught us that humility is a virtue and, as educators, we are the role models needed and required to champion this. What we do mean, however, is the absolute deserved recognition that you are a person of great value and merit with the daunting responsibility to lead others. It is possible to honor yourself while remaining humble and modest. So exactly what do we mean by honoring yourself?

Honoring yourself means getting in touch with yourself. It means knowing who you are and, more importantly, who you are not. It is learning to trust what you value and knowing that others have no misunderstanding of that. You are not wishy-washy in what you believe and have the ability to make a realistic assessment of who you are and where you want to go both personally and professionally and why. You can self-assess.

Daniel Goleman (1998), in his article entitled, *What Makes a Leader?*, clearly explains *self-awareness*, one of the five components of emotional intelligence at work. Without such a component, a leader who lacks self-awareness is likely to make decisions and or policies that bring about turmoil and upheaval rather than harmony and agreement.

Honoring yourself means getting better and growing each year in the position because daily situations and challenges provide fertile ground for such growth and development, as no two days are ever alike. Watch and be happily surprised as you see your proficiency grow in building, managing, and extending school relationships and witness the growth in your special strengths and talents you bring to the school setting.

Honoring yourself means that you do need to take the time to feel good about yourself and what you stand for. Even more so, you must take the time to respect and admire your own work, your own being and all that you accomplish in our noble field. You must remain mentally healthy in order to be an effective leader and for others to be guided, influenced and positively affected by you. A main responsibility of a leader is building relationships—being a relationship specialist. To do so, you need to be mentally healthy yourself and feel good about what you are doing, have done, and will do. This chapter provides suggestions in three primary areas: reflection, protection and skill, and attribute selection. So, just what are we talking about here?

A visit to Washington, DC usually includes a trip to the Lincoln Memorial and the Washington Monument. One can't help but notice the austere Lincoln Memorial Reflecting Pool reflecting both these famous monuments. Although it is extremely unlikely that we will never see monuments erected to us, we can certainly use the symbolism of the reflecting pool to ponder who we are, how we come across to others, our chosen profession, and all that we do that is right and just.

In addition, we all know the importance of protecting our loved ones, our students, and even ourselves. Our first thoughts usually go to physical protection but we also realize that we have the daunting responsibility to provide mental and emotional protection. This chapter ponders tips that will help you protect your sense of honor, mental well being if you will, during those tough and challenging times.

Lastly, educational philosophies abound with the desire to transform our students into life-long learners. If we can just instill in our students and those we lead the passion and desire to learn for learning's sake, we will have accomplished much. So, too, there are skills and attributes you can learn, if you haven't already done so, and put into practice. This chapter provides suggestions on recognizing and acquiring a set of skills and attributes that will assist you in maintaining your ability to feel positive, even wonderful for that matter, about yourself. A skill and attribute set that will help shield you during questionable feelings of self-doubt and self-worth throughout those all too often taxing times.

Honoring yourself is a gift you can give yourself, and certainly one worth taking. You might view it as a gift of improved self-esteem so that you can function better and evolve into an exemplary school leader. Honoring who you are, your values and needs, can model for others how worthwhile an educator's life can be. In the end, we hope you will have acquired the necessary positive outlook on your own professional life to realize your importance, value, self-worth, and accomplishments.

Arrange Your Environment So It Reflects You.

We live in a world where our environment is more at risk than ever. As a global society, we have become more concerned and more attentive to environmental problems like greenhouse emissions, global warming, acid rain, hazardous waste, water pollution, and rainforest destruction. For our sake and for our children and their children's sake, we need to be more protective, observant, and vigilant of our environment.

In like manner, albeit without the potential for catastrophe, we should be very protective, observant, and vigilant of our own environment—our personal workspace. You see, your personal workspace, be it your classroom or your office, reflects and sends an ever-constant and timeless message about who you are and what you stand for. It oozes the person you have become, your educational philosophy, belief system, abilities, and strengths, and, yes, even your weaknesses. Your environment is your mirror image that tells people all about you without you ever having to be there.

Although I didn't know it at the time, my first fifth grade classroom in 1972 said who I was to the parents and my children when they first stepped foot in *my* room. For example *my* bulletin board, which I am embarrassed to say took up the back of the entire classroom read, "Try It You'll Like It." Large words that spanned an entire wall replete with the text "Mathematics," "Language Arts," "Social Studies," and "Science." By October *we* had moved the desks around the edge of the room, opened up the center of the room for learning and placed a carpet there, and displayed a handwritten sign in front of each child that one of the students had produced for all of *us*. It was a quote I remember being passed down from my grandmother:

Your greatness is measured by your kindness.

Your education by your modesty.

Your real caliber is measured by the consideration and tolerance you have for others.

The year 1983 would see me as a superintendent/principal with a rather large office that had a conference table. How did I arrange the space, use it, and decorate it? Virtually every item had meaning, function, and message-sending potential. My colleague superintendents would liken coming to my office for an annual superintendents meeting to going on a "field trip"—too much to see, too much to do. Following are some of the noticeable things I did that reflected on me that was constantly sending messages to the public:

The superintendent's personal parking space—My first action as a superintendent was to dig out the sign and throw it in the garbage.

The desk—I moved it from an obscure corner in the office where the public could not view it to a space by the door where everyone could see it and me (for the little time I spent in the office).

The eagles—Our mascot was an eagle so I started an eagle collection. Any eagle from anyone who gave one to me, in any format, was displayed.

Family pictures—My family pictures were prominently on display.

The walls—I filled them with pictures, notes, and items students had given me and secured them to the wall with masking tape. It was cluttered and messy. I asked my art teacher to work with the students and paint a mural on the north wall of my office. There was so much "stuff" everywhere that my board president walked in during my first month on the job and said that she thought we better frame and hang my PhD diploma from Northwestern University, the implication being so people would at least know I was legitimate. I framed it and placed it on the wall behind my desk. The wall eventually became replete with framed documents, plaques, and items reflecting my entitlement to the job. In a way, it gave me legitimacy to do the things I wanted to do.

The conference table and chairs in my office—Under my administration they were used by teachers for meetings, board members for closed sessions, and even birthday celebrations and lunches by the support staff. With so many people frequenting the office, I felt I was always in the loop and knew what was going on. Oh, the tables and chairs were old but functional. I wasn't going to spend a dime to put in fancy new furniture, or even a new rug.

The saltwater aquarium—A former student set up a 75-gallon tank and the children enjoyed coming in the office and seeing it and feeding the fish and corals from time to time.

This worked for me. I hope that both my classroom in 1972 and my office until 2007, were both functional and gave the following message: "I am legitimate, child centered, open, approachable, and, most importantly, care, and care deeply." I remember the village manager telling me during a visit my first year that the office certainly looked like I planned on being there a while. I was. One disclaimer: Certainly my style has its limits on transfer and for some people, maybe most people, parts of what I do would be dead wrong. My office was very cluttered. Some would say a cluttered office is a cluttered mind. I would say they are right and this is one of my weaknesses. My only point is that *you* should conduct an environmental audit to see what messages *you* are sending regularly to anyone who can view your home at work. As my friends at *Instructor Magazine* taught me, you never get a second chance to make a good first impression.

Be Upfront, Close, and Personal When Choosing Your Heroes.

Traditional heroes, the ones we celebrate, admire, and talk about, come in different sizes and shapes and can be of any gender, race, and ethnicity. I bet you could easily name a nationally recognized hero who would fall into one of the following categories: history, sports, movie and TV stars, authors, religion, medicine, music, art, science, business, and, yes, even education. Your names might include the likes of Abraham Lincoln, Eleanor Roosevelt, Albert Einstein, Martin Luther King, Jr., Marie Curie, Tiger Woods, Beethoven, and, yes, perhaps even John Dewey.

Although these people, and so many others, certainly have carved out their hero niche, they are people you can only see and hear via avenues such as movies, books, and TV shows—unless, of course, you happen to bump into the likes of a Michael Jordan. With all the problems that plague potential 21st century heroes these days, it has been said that there are very few left to choose from. For decades now I have preferred my heroes to remain local—to be people I can see and touch. People who are a stone's throw away from me and people with whom I can talk, learn from first-hand, and, ultimately, model myself after. So where are these people anyway? I contend they are all around us—either in part or in whole (explained later), and you just have to find them. The following are some of my heroes and their stories.

Growing up I watched my parents struggle every day to make ends meet. I witnessed my mom transition from being an opera singer with the D'Oyly Carte Opera Company in London to cleaning bathrooms in the apartment building my parents managed. I watched my dad battle cancer, be operated on, have 150 stitches, and return to work the very next day driving a forty-foot semitractor-trailer.

In college I admired my "Music 101" teacher. I remember her taking me aside and telling me in a kind and gentle manner the bad news. She told me I sang off-key every time and scored the lowest of any student she had ever taught on her comprehensive music pretest. She respected the fact that I was involved in a lot of service projects on campus and, as such, decided to give me private singing lessons. In the end though, she told me sing softly—some people are just tone deaf.

As an elementary teacher I looked up to the first principal who hired me, Dr. John Beckwith. I remember his comment the day he offered me the job. He wasn't convinced what I knew about teaching but he was completely sure about my enthusiasm and hard work ethic. He has been a guiding force to this day.

While working on my PhD, Dr. William Hazard became my hero. I remember his continuous and unwavering support. One time I was worried as my wife and I were new parents and paying 100% of Northwestern's tuition costs. He told me that he was certain I would finish and not to worry. He also said for me not to let the bureaucratic red tape get me down. He was a mentor until his death a few years ago. His memory will always assist me.

As a principal I found Rick Walters, a sixth grade teacher, to be my hero. He exemplified all that is good and great in our profession. He traveled the farthest of any teacher in my school and was frequently the first one there in the morning. I even caught him there many times on Sundays. He worked hard to differentiate his instruction and bring out the best in each and every child. I have a card he wrote me that I keep on my dresser just to remind me of him.

As my career progressed and I became a superintendent I modeled myself after the likes of Drs. William Attea (an incredibly hard worker who rarely slept), Charles Young (who was smart and statesmanlike), Peg Lee (kind, caring, and a class act), and Homer Harvey (a man of utmost compassion), as well as school board members like Fred Gouger (a moral and ethical giant). You see, you can take people whole or in part. I learned to disaggregate the best traits in the people with whom my path crossed. I tried to take the best from each of them and make them part of me. Even now at the university I model myself after Dr. Ken Addison, a brilliant, empathetic, humorous, calm, and caring professor. You see, in our profession it shouldn't be hard to look next door and find someone local who has at least one trait worthy of hero status.

Model yourself after people you can gaze your eyes upon and experience everyday—someone you can touch and actually get an autograph from, or someone you have been in association with over the years. Because it is firsthand and, as such, a primary source, it will be easier to learn their great traits and become better yourself by modeling the personal heroes right next door to you. Ones that are living and breathing because seeing is truly believing.

In short, you need heroes who are real, alive, and not far from you—even fallible if you will. Educators who will make you feel proud to be in our profession, consistently remind you why you became a school leader and who will be honored as you model yourself after their worthy traits. In time you will pay it forward and be just like that person you modeled. After all, imitation is the highest form of flattery.

Celebrate Your Versatility.

I believe the older one gets, the more reflective one becomes. Maybe it's because one enjoys the "good old days" or maybe as one gets older one has more memories to reflect upon than time left to make new ones. I'm not sure. With so many other professions out there from which to choose, I do know that I have frequently reflected on the path that led me to become a school leader. We have all come to become educators in various ways and by various means and via various mentors, friends and/or acquaintances. Each of us has a special and unique story of our journey in becoming an educational leader. For all of us I would bet it began with a fundamental belief that contributing to our youth was a just and noble contribution to humanity. For me the journey began as a psychology major and being in a service fraternity (Alpha Phi Omega) and my "brothers" convincing me that I would make a very good teacher after seeing me work with children during our service projects. Although I had completed all the requirements for my psychology degree save one, I was open to changing majors as I thought that I might not make for a good psychologist because how could I help solve other people's problems when I had way too many problems of my own to solve. One thing led to another, as I am sure it did for you, and I became an educator. I have continually asked myself where am I today and where am I on that journey.

One thing I learned along the way was that the role of a school leader is so diverse that it requires the skill set of a multitude of people from a multitude of careers. We have commonly joked in our profession that we are fireman and policeman at times. But we do act on a stage, handle medical needs of students, resolve conflicts, investigate and gather evidence on problems, care for the environment, and so on and so on. As such, just think about the general skill set required in the following occupations and how that skill set may have been used by you in your role as an educational leader recently: accountant, actor, architect, artist, body guard, CEO, clergy (minister, priest, rabbi, etc.), contractor, designer, detective, dentist, doctor, ecologist, editor, engineer, game show host, handyman, judge, lawyer, nanny, pilot, plumber, playwright, psychiatrist, public relations spokesperson, receptionist, scientist, sculptor, social worker, and writer.

It goes without saying that there is a little tongue-in-check here with writing such an exhaustive list and that we couldn't just walk into any of these jobs off the street. These professions are separate, distinct, and unique—requiring in some cases extensive years of training. But what I am attempting to convey here is that the basic fundamental image, the one-liner job description if you may, from these professions could easily cover many of the tasks we, as school leaders, do every day. And I am sure I have certainly missed a number of occupations that I could have listed.

We deserve recognition for the complexity of our work as we migrate the landscape of our jobs everyday. It's a tough road we hoe. Rejoice in your talents and your ability to multitask. Be happy that you have such a diverse skill set. And recognize that your abilities are broad based, versatile, and most deserving of respect.

Connect the Dots.

One of my favorite activities as a youngster was buying one of those connect-the-dots books, grabbing a pencil and connecting the dots on the page. Drawing a line carefully from one number to another in sequence created a picture. But one page was never enough. Several pages had to be attempted, and if time permitted, they could even be colored. Satisfaction came when all the dots were connected in succession and the image appeared. If the dots were not done in the correct order the picture did not look precise. I would end up with a crazy fish or teapot, but the good news was I could always erase or redirect my marker line, correct my mistake, and move on.

Connecting the dots in the work of a school leader can be seen as a road map to achieving goals and success. It can be the big picture, small picture, or several pictures on several pages needing attention and connection simultaneously. I think of connecting the dots with the goal of completing the big picture as articulating a vision and following the dots sequentially as the mission evolves and unfolds. Sometimes we get stuck and have to regroup or retrace our steps. That is normal.

So think of dots as being good, like good friends. Dots are valuable because they are the benchmarks, signposts, and mile markers that help us get closer to the image or the goal of our work. If we skip dots the image is incomplete, distorted and we have to regroup. When we fail to connect the dots for educators, there is disengagement, misinterpretation of what is expected, and confusion. Sometimes the "buy-in" we were hoping for disappears. The dots are critical because they play a key role and guide us, but it takes the skills of a leader to make the picture come together.

You should take the time to plan and strategically place the dots so you can anticipate the more difficult steps that others might encounter along the way and how you will support them. If you go zigzagging, inconsistently making followers dizzy, eventually they will become disconnected, discouraged and drop out. Dot acceleration can come only after confidence that everyone is on the "same page."

But, don't be shy about moving to the next dot. You have probably heard teachers say the following:

Why are we doing this?

This too will pass.

If we wait long enough, another idea will drop out of the sky and replace this one.

My plate is full.

Past experiences can make educators reluctant about trying new things and they may even want to convince you not to progress but stay stuck on one comfortable dot. In actuality, they may not be paying attention. Keep moving forward while the actions and reactions of others will give you notice if you have strayed off the beaten path.

School stakeholders may be different in the way they perceive the dots and the likeness of the goals, but you can meet their needs and redraw the image together if needed. For instance, so much of the work in curriculum development, facilitation, implementation, and evaluation involves dot-to-dot pages. One page might be the committee developing, altering, or redesigning the technology curriculum. Another page might be the pilot committee working to try out new innovations in technology before the improvement is adopted unilaterally. There might be a page or committee to evaluate and adjust what was initially created and all of these are processes and dots with the main picture waiting to be filled in—a new curriculum or program for students. Trust that you have the skills to successfully design and connect a dotted road map. You will navigate, communicate, interpret, and make connections for success.

Create Your Own Wristband.

On January 8, 1985, I was in the Expectant Father's Waiting Room at Lutheran General Hospital listening to, not watching, the television. The news story of the day was Elvis Presley's fiftieth birthday and his legacy. I was pacing the floor and anxiously awaiting the birth of our third child. Suddenly, in the room next door, I overheard one of the doctors say, "Oh, you have two boys and now you have another one." Having two sons already, my thoughts immediately changed from the hopes of a "daddy's girl" to the beginning of a basketball dynasty. Well, as it turned out, the comment was for the guy next to me. Later on when the doctor told me that I was the proud father of a newborn girl, well, that was, without question, one of the happiest moments in my life. I remember the challenge of trying to find "her" covered in a pink blanket in the nursery. The color ruled out about half of the competition. I then found myself squinting to find "her" last name on a card. With it being the first day of her life, her last name would be the only visible identifying factor.

Most of us come into this world with a hospital bracelet, a blue or pink blanket, a knitted cap, and a last name. With the probable exception of our DNA, our identity is a true "tabula rasa" which, as each minute passes, will begin to take shape, form, and substance. Pretty soon our parents will bestow upon us a first name (we chose Stephanie), and, perhaps, a middle name and more. Eventually we will be issued a hospital birth certificate with our very own distinct footprint because our unique fingerprint is not ready for processing yet. There will be many other identifiable characteristics unique to only us, starting with items such as a government issued social security card with our own number. Then there will be other idiosyncratic markings as we get older like student ID cards, a driver's license, and perhaps even a passport. In addition, we have our own voice identification pattern, retina for scanning, and dental records. In our technology-driven global society we also acquire our very own email address and all those personalized passwords that we have to remember. In short, *you*, become *you* and, as I told my daughter, there is only one *you*.

As a classroom teacher we learn the value and importance of routines. Children come to know us and what to expect from us. This is a valuable teaching skill. A similar pattern holds true for *you* as a colleague. As a school leader, the people you work with come to learn who *you* are, what makes *you* tick, what *you* stand for, how *you* will act and react, and what *you* expect with and from them. For the most part *you* become credible and predictable. As a school leader, the people with whom *you* work should know *you* so well that they can act in your stead. I am not saying they can be *you*, as we know that is not possible, but they can learn to think as *you* would think, act as *you* would act, react as *you* would react, and follow through on items as *you* would. The following is a case in point.

Mike was my district's facility manager. He was a man of great intelligence and work ethic, who loved to read poetry to the younger children or teach astronomy to the older ones. But, alas, he was the facility manager who, on occasion, did need a gentle reminder of his primary job. After working with me for a year, he realized that written reports better be accurate in nature and near perfect, using correct grammar conventions and good word choice. After experiencing a couple of marked up reports, Mike's work was as if I wrote it (if not better!). He knew exactly what I wanted, how I wanted it, and when it needed to be completed. I was going to name this tip "Be Like Mike," but thought it might be too confusing with Michael Jordan.

Like it or not every day that the sun sets will find that you have added to your own wristband for others to wear. Livestrong, WWJD (What Would Jesus Do), mother's bracelets, POW (Prisoner of War) bracelets and others may get you comments, questions, and/or great discussions, but the identity bracelet you create with your thinking, actions, words, and deeds, albeit never worn, will be the one your colleagues remember and take to the bank. Unlike the horrors associated with identity theft, *you* want "identity theft" to occur here. Yes, *you* want people to understand *you* and be able to act like *you*. I am not saying become a "mini-me"; I am saying that your colleagues should learn to value and respect *you* and think and act in a similar manner. In short, your bracelet, WW (*your name initial here*) D is there for everyone in your school to wear. Imitating *you* will either be the highest form of flattery or the lowest form of leader compliance. The only question is, what will your bracelet stand for?

Embody Your School.

Sometime during your tenure of leadership *it* happens. You take on the identity of the school, department, team, grade level, or group that you are leading. In some ways *it* could be called real identity transfer because people begin to refer to you as the institution, department, team, or group. For instance, you become the English Department at Great Expectations High School or the Language Arts Team at Climbing Ivy Middle School, or the principal at Park Elementary School. I have even had people slip up and introduce me as, "Dr. Bush, Orland Park School." You represent, symbolize, and embody that group, as well as who you are as a person. People see you in this role and assigned position and attach the group to you. When you attend meetings inside the school district or outside in the community you are yourself, but at the same time you are representing many others. It is like having a Zen experience without losing your uniqueness. Some might call it *becoming one* with the institution whether you like it or not.

Individuals who bike long distances talk of *becoming one with their bike.* It is that euphoric, effortless experience of riding a bike and working as one unit. But it must also be said that not every experience—or in this case riding a bike—is a *becoming one experience.* It takes work and constant practice. Teachers, parents, and students can perceive this *oneness with the institution* through your leadership style, tone, body language, skills, and relationships, as well as by how you implement and embody the core beliefs and premises of the mission of the school.

Let's take diversity as an example of embodiment and the concept of *oneness.* Many school mission statements talk about honoring and meeting the needs of a diverse community. I have observed school leaders who honor diversity by having the right conversations about respecting the differences among students as to ethnicity, academic performance, and needs, and following through with "the talk in their everyday walk" as evidenced in decision making and problem solving for students. Saying must be followed by doing in leadership in order to be considered educational embodiment.

Honor yourself by *becoming one with the institution.* Demonstrate those behaviors, competencies and skills that embody, engage and exemplify the meaning of the mission of the school and personify spirit, sport, kindness, academic performance, effort and caring for teachers, students, and parents. Be a tireless champion or cheerleader for what your school stands for and eliminate those elements that do not reflect the values of the school such as disrespect, intolerance, and/or negativity. It has been my experience that the longer you stay in your leadership position the more individuals will perceive *becoming one* with you, your values, and your mission. Don't be surprised if others begin to imitate you. Maybe it will not happen in every situation everyday, but it is a goal worth pursuing.

Establish an Anecdotal File on Yourself.

Educators use anecdotal files as tools for a variety of reasons. Usually they are paper files that collect miscellaneous information for later use. These files contain notes, discussions, agreements, disciplinary and remedial contractual terms about employees who report to you, logs of things to remember such as buses that are consistently late or a conversation that is held at a precise date and time. They are simple, personal, and help us remember by providing a paper trail for future use.

We frequently write notes to ourselves because of the enormous amount of interactions and incidents that take place during a school day. These files jog our memories so we don't forget things when we are on brain overload. Anecdotal records may even be used in an employee due process hearing when specific dates, times, and details are necessary to remember.

While these customary folders are sitting in your desk, we would suggest starting a different type of anecdotal file—one about yourself. Start by saving things that are given to you during the day; greeting cards that say thank you or the parent who writes you a note about what a great year his or her youngster had at school. Emails also count and so do kind words in the form of thank you notes, ragged slips of paper or Post-it notes, quotes, bookmarks, funny cartoons, photographs, and student work. Don't forget to include positive newspaper articles about you and your school if they are meaningful to you. File away these items for future reference.

One item I put in my file was a note to myself not to forget about a kindergarten boy who brought a butcher knife for show and tell. (You cannot make up these real life stories!) Or the first grader who had had enough of school one day, pushed open the school door and decided to walk home with the entire community looking for him for hours. Then there was the photo of the giant U.S. rainbow-colored map on the playground that the construction company painted incorrectly (they forgot Georgia). All these incidents are funny now, not so funny at the time; however, they certainly earned a place in my anecdotal file.

These collectibles help us recall and remember those surprise moments when someone took the time to write us and compliment us on our work. Others make us chuckle, laugh out loud, or break down the tension we are feeling. Luckily, you won't be asked to produce your personal anecdotal file in court. There is no mediation, hearings, advocates, lawyers, or due process to worry about. There is no reason to even purge it for inappropriate language, name calling, or nonsense. It is refreshing, positive, harmless, and easily worth the time it took to create.

The real purpose of this file about you is quick therapy, attitude adjustment, and/or just plain fun. When you have had a bad day, people are stressing you out or you are working alone on a Saturday, you might want to reach for this file in your desk and take a quick read. Surprisingly, like an aspirin that works to relieve a headache, school life falls back into perspective. Create an anecdotal file to remind yourself why you signed up for this job.

Ground Yourself in Reflective Thinking.

What went wrong today? What went right?
How can I improve that situation?
Tomorrow I am going to try this strategy.
That was a thoughtless thing to say to that teacher.
Did I consider all the alternatives to that problem?
Am I home from school already? How did I get here?

Today's school leaders have so many demands, pressures, and interruptions—both assigned and self-imposed—that they are regularly working on overload. Sometimes surviving is the most important goal, not really noticing where they are, where they are going next or who they are becoming as leaders. I can hear some school leaders say, "Time to reflect.... You've got to be kidding. I hardly have time to go to the bathroom or eat lunch!" Finding opportunities and time to reflect on leadership work appears to be a luxury for some, yet the value of reflection alone and with others is noteworthy. Availing oneself of reflection opportunities can only serve to make our work better as professionals when we review, analyze, redesign and restructure our ideas and actions through intentional thought.

It is interesting to think about where we reflect—waiting at a stop light, crawling in traffic, driving the car to work thinking about the day ahead, on the way home thinking about the day that unfolded, standing in the checkout line, sitting in the doctor's office, watching a sports event, attending a dull meeting or listening to monotonous speaker. We are mentally available and ready to ponder.

Everyone needs regular opportunities for self renewal and growing in reflection can yield many benefits. Being grounded by thinking deeply about what we do everyday leads to asking better questions, breaking ineffective routines, and yielding better solutions to urgent problems. It allows you to engage in thought based on your professional experience. You can see if your actions are in concert with your values and beliefs. Reflection allows you time to step back and take a panoramic view of the world in which you work. For example you might reflect on whether or not a reduction-in-force (RIF) situation is really necessary in the big picture as it effects the quality of education for the students in your school. You might want to mentally rehearse the conversation with a parent who is defending their child in a recent fistfight or how to make a faculty meeting better. Additionally, it can be effective to reflect in a group setting, such as several leaders responding to the same question, "What do you like most about your job?" Conducting a school leader reflection audit is a productive use of time because it is a form of checks and balances to see if your values and actions are aligned, consistent, and demonstrate excellence with how you are performing.

Henry David Thoreau says, "In our fast-paced society perhaps one of the greatest missing ingredients is the act of reflection, of slowing down, of being deliberate thinkers" (http://www.ecostudies.org/syefest/aplres13.htm). Can you slow down (mentally and physically) and allow yourself to let your mind take you wherever it wants to or really mull over an issue? Can you afford not to go on a mental reflection vacation?

Juggle with Scarves Before You Try Torches.

In the juggling world, technical skills are necessary to dazzle the audience with one's performance and its level of difficulty. Sometimes we see the juggler start slowly with one ball in the air, then two, then three, and then a circle of balls going faster and higher. We are amazed and stunned at the precision of balance and risk involved. In the school leader world, juggling is a metaphor for learning on the job: juggling duties, expectations, demands, roles, and hats, faster, higher, better. The school leader juggles not only tasks, but a long list of roles such as administrator, negotiator, school comptroller, disciplinarian, counselor, instructional leader, assessment expert, facilities manager, and colleague. School leadership may look easy enough at first, but as the days go by many concerns are left up in the air, such as time demands, heavy workloads, and family.

One school juggling example that comes to mind is in the area of supervision and evaluation of personnel. Keeping everything in balance during the supervision and evaluation process can be as difficult as juggling with torches or, better yet, sharp knives. It can be a fine line or the delicate balance between success and disaster with those who are being supervised and evaluated by you. A school leader needs to follow the school district policies, and federal and state laws, rules, and regulations, while at the same time promoting personnel professional growth and development within a supportive school environment—sticky, tricky, and risky.

When juggling work expectations, begin slowly, like novice jugglers do with scarves, carefully honing your skills and then taking a more daring step, but take that step. Watch for patterns and routines such as central office walkthroughs so you can improve your skills and fulfill your role expectations. Observe PTO fundraising events so you can gain a greater command and awareness of the supportive work done by parents. Additionally, beware: everyone in the audience is watching you.

School leaders sometimes worry that someone might notice when a ball falls to the ground. As a principal and the mother of two small children I worried about meeting my leadership expectations and family obligations. I worried about what would happen if my babysitter got sick and I had to scramble before my school day started to find a new sitter for my children and possibly be late to work. I worried about who would be able to take my daughter to gymnastics or pick up my son from soccer practice twice a week. Because I viewed my roles as a privilege (mother and school principal), I worried that I was "dropping the ball" on something, and, of course, I did. From the juggle, you learn more from the drops than the catches. But most of all I learned not to be hard on myself when I "dropped the ball" because learning and risk taking are symbiotic natural processes.

From struggling in juggling, go to risk taking and translating mistakes into new ways of learning in order to push yourself to the next level. For instance, try to push yourself to another level of performance that might appear impossible at first, like writing for a grant to fund a special project when maybe you have never tried grant writing before. Throw the scarf up, not so high as to lose control, but at just the right height to catch it and throw the next one up until the scarves flow in harmony in the air. Move to more challenging tasks (balls, rings, and torches) as your confidence grows. Having learned from your mistakes, getting your work done will become more efficient and effective. Satisfaction in juggling comes in the form of more self-awareness and confidence. Start slow—with scarves—but start. Move from level to level before you try torches. Having a positive mental attitude, neither overbearing nor overconfident, just like the professional juggler, will improve your odds of success.

Keep Your Perspective.

Have you ever taken a class that you just didn't "get?" You know the one where no matter how hard you studied, no matter how hard you worked, the information just wouldn't sink in. I remember my freshman year at Gordon Technical High School in Chicago. Just off the bat I should have seen failure written all over the word "technical" as I am clearly not and greatly admire those who are. Every freshman was required to take a mechanical drawing class. I quickly concluded that I was low man on the totem pole in that class. I just couldn't do multiple-view perspective drawings and repeatedly looked for assistance from my friend who just happened to be the second lowest scoring person on that totem pole. I have heard the term "failure with dignity," but rest assured there was no dignity in those repeated failings for me. I just didn't have the skill-set to visualize the perspective that was required to do those drawings. I didn't then, and don't today for that matter. I don't have the intellectual capacity for architectural perspective.

Perspective, however, comes in different sizes and shapes. *Situational perspective*, the ability to evaluate a situation, that is, to have an understanding of that situation, to be able to view the variables and the facets that encompass that situation, is a much-needed and required skill as an educational leader. To be able to analyze, prioritize, and synthesize situations that are brought to our attention, and frequently brought with passion and vigor, is an ability school leaders must develop and continue to nurture in order to survive. The development of educational leadership perspective should include being factual and analytical, as well as, in general, being free of emotion.

In our roles we face a constant barrage of concerns and problems that to the persons presenting them usually hit the top of *their* priority list. After a while *their* problems can also involve a multitude of other people—and people frequently taking sides and making the problem even bigger. I dealt with a testing scandal once, words the television media would use; I prefer the state board's determination that it was a testing irregularity—although that sounded like I needed a laxative. State exam student test answer booklets had been altered and the students were the ones who discovered the problem and blew the whistle on it. The students were the real heroes in this ordeal and that was ultimately duly noted in a *Chicago Tribune* editorial. They had real character for stepping forward. But the problems created by this ordeal involved many "characters" and were significant, time-consuming, and required the skills of a detective, rabbi, priest, minister, politician, peacemaker, and collaborator. Most importantly it required me to keep my perspective at times when parents, teachers, students, the community at large, and the news media each independently had their own perspective. Notice I am saying *their* perspective, not a mistaken perspective, just *their* perspective. The keeping of one's perspective requires one to remain open, analytical, persistent, emotion free, open to new information, calm, cool and collected as well as leader-like in all deliberations. What was challenging about this particular problem was that the superintendent—that would be me—had the appearance to many as having the most to gain from altered higher test scores. Being a main suspect while simultaneously trying to solve the problem requires an extra dose of even-keeled perspective. As the first week into the crisis concluded, a teacher resigned and life slowly, very slowly, returned to normal. No one ever confessed. No one was ever found guilty.

It's times like this that faith in yourself and belief in the fundamental purpose of our mission and goals for students give you strength. In the end, one thing I learned was that the vast majority of problems we deal with, although not this one, have a short shelf life. They come and they go and with them are very few casualties.

People either bring their emotion-laden problems to us for solving or in the course of our business the problems wind up at our doorstep. We need to keep our unbiased perspective when attempting to solve them, and must remember that there are few things that will be remembered from those meetings. Even the ones that are very significant at the time lose their luster and meaning over time. What doesn't lose its luster is how *you* handled the problem and kept your perspective. How *you* kept your focus on being an independent thinker with the tenacity to grind it out. When migrating the challenges of individual and group concerns, whether with a parent, at a school board meeting, or with a colleague, I learned to ask myself one question, "What will people really remember next month?"

Laugh at Yourself.

A delightful parent of two bright and charming children came to see me one day. She said that she was very pleased with her children's education and my role as her children's principal. I did get to know her quite well over the years. She then looked me in the eyes and said how worried she was about me. I asked her why. She simply referred me to my drinking problem. I was dumbfounded and asked her why she thought I had a drinking problem. She said she had learned of it first-hand. Now I was really wondering what was going on. Sure I enjoyed a couple of glasses of beer or wine now and then but that was it. Did I have a twin out there (pity that person) who drank too much? No. She went on to tell me that whenever she calls me on the telephone her caller ID brings up "Schols " (pronounced s hōōl s) Pub." I am half English and she was Australian. Maybe she had heard of my pubcrawl when I was in Oxford. After all I think Australian pubs were descendants of English pubs. Who knows how many people she had shared my suspected drinking problem with? Then it dawned on me; the light bulb went on. Wait a minute, I said. "Schols Pub" must be the phone company's abbreviation for "Schools Public." That is what came up on her caller ID when she telephoned me. We both couldn't stop laughing. I am sure there was some damage control to be done but eventually the truth would come out and, yes, sometimes you just have to laugh. My first instinct with most problems like this is to laugh, laugh hard, and realize that our jobs are so "public," no pun intended here, that we better not take ourselves too seriously. Others do take us seriously and frequently watch, analyze, and microfiche our actions, words, and deeds. But if we join them, fear can easily set in.

School events provide us the opportunity to laugh at ourselves and not take ourselves too seriously. Now I am not suggesting that you should be a clown everyday. I am only saying that certain situations lend themselves to laughter, being on the lighter side, and laughing at ourselves if you will. These situations may be by design or they may happen by accident. For example, as a classroom teacher, when Halloween came around, I, like many of you have probably done, would wear a costume to school, such as Winnie the Pooh. I was even Dorothy one year when my team dressed up in the *Wizard of Oz* theme. One of my students even taught me how to be a plainclothes policeman. Michael, a tremendously gifted student in the 1970s, did not have his costume (or so I thought) for Halloween one year. I offered to drive him home at lunch (something we couldn't do now by the way) to get it. He said, Mr. B., I have my costume on; can't you tell I'm a plainclothes policeman. I learned to use that line.

Even my very first year teaching, and every teaching year thereafter, found me dressed as Santa for the annual holiday staff school breakfast. Some of my colleagues, from custodians to teachers, were Santa's reindeers, angels, elves, and even sugar plum fairies. It was an enjoyable time and we certainly started the day in good spirits.

Then there was the dunk tank. I never missed an opportunity to be in the dunk tank. It began as a teacher then continued for 27 years as an administrator; I really enjoyed it. I know—I am sick. Who would enjoy getting dunked by a bunch of children (and even some adults)? As the school superintendent/principal, I chose to wear a suit, white shirt, tie, shoes, "Ringling Brothers Barnum and Bailey" circus lapel pin—the whole nine yards—to get dunked. The children loved it. What could be better than dunking their principal with his suit on? The first dunk was always the best. However, I was worried near the end of my career that the lines might get too long (what a great shot for disgruntled parents or that child who didn't get that A). They didn't. I am not saying my actions are right for you; for most people they are not. I am just saying keep it light. Keep your spirits up. Laugh at yourself and others will laugh with you—not at you. You will develop a reputation of being an enjoyable person, with life in perspective and one that is approachable. Learn what is the right level of humor for you, and employ it.

It is common knowledge about the health benefits of laughter. But beyond the health benefits there is another benefit that I think is even more important. Humility. Never take yourself too seriously. We can all be replaced in a heartbeat. So, in the meantime, enjoy life and realize that if others see you laughing, displaying your sense of humor, and laughing at yourself, who knows, they may even learn to do it, too.

Learn to Take a Compliment.

Howard and I talked about this tip when we were considering putting it in this book. We both admitted to having great difficulty learning to accept a professional compliment. How can taking a compliment be so difficult for us, and other school leaders for that matter, and worthy of mention in our book?

In our cases, we suffer from an affliction that we nicknamed *compliment transfer*. This misfortune can best be described as an ability to quickly transfer the kind words stemming from a compliment to someone else, thus declining and deflecting any reference of the compliment at all. *Compliment transfer* is explained and highlighted in the following scenario:

A parent approaches you and compliments you on a wonderful end-of-the-year assembly. You quickly point out that the students were the ones who made the assembly so special because of their accomplishments and the teachers organized the event, and created a wonderful theme for the assembly, and the parent organization provided the refreshments that would feed an army, and (without taking a breath) the students have such wonderful parents that it's easy to see your support in their work.

Although this example is true, what my parents wanted to hear is just a simple, "thank you." Instead I would tend to go on and on about others to the point that the listener sometimes wondered if I had any participation in the event at all. Sometimes because of our inability to accept compliments our humble words shrug off the compliment and our involvement, allowing the listener to form incorrect opinions about us.

When I was in my fifth year of teaching, Joan Goodwin, my principal, taught me the value of learning to acknowledge, accept, and graciously handle a compliment. During my evaluations she would compliment me on my teaching. I would feel awkward, red-faced, look at the ground, and transfer the conversation kudos to something else. Occasionally, I would be quick to correct her by saying, "You just came on a good day" or "I was lucky today, several students were absent." Having heard enough of my deflections, Joan took me aside and said, "Lynn, when someone compliments you, look them in the eye and just say, *thank you*, nothing more is needed. Just a simple *thank you* is all that people are expecting to hear, not the laundry list of excuses why you aren't deserving of the compliment."

The art of accepting a compliment is truly a skill some need to learn. Acknowledging the work you have had a hand in is an opportunity to show and model for others your gracefulness. School leaders need to learn to take a compliment not only because they deserve it but also because they are acknowledging the legitimacy, kindness, understanding, and thoughtfulness of the person delivering the compliment. Or you can think of it another way. If you keep telling others often enough that you don't deserve credit, eventually they might believe you.

Leave a Forwarding Address.

Like many people, I worked numerous jobs before finishing my undergraduate studies. Twelve to be exact, but who's counting. Money was scarce and I paid all my own expenses. My parents moved numerous times from one apartment to another. I remember taking the Greyhound bus home my freshman year from Northern Illinois University to downtown Chicago followed by the "EL" ride to an apartment a couple miles from Wrigley Field. After that, I walked about a mile from the "EL" to the apartment with my suitcase; I was pretty tired. I walked to the apartment door only to find the following note on it: "Dear son, we moved." I knew my parents loved me though because they left the forwarding address taped to the front door. I schlepped my way a few miles west down the road to the next apartment and really laughed and remembered thinking "now that's pretty funny." Many years later I got my dad a father's day card that remarked about the fun games of hide and seek we used to play. The card went something like this: the front of the card said, " Remember those fun games of Hide N' Seek we used to play. I would hide my eyes, count to 100." The inside of the card read, "and you and mom would pack up and move away."

Change, whether it be places or jobs, is life altering. Most of us will move places and change jobs during the course of our lifetime. It has been said that the average person changes careers, not just jobs, but careers, three times. What is important though is what we do during our "stay." During the course of that "stay" we will make friends and exert our leader influence. That's what leaders do—they influence others. We do what we can to get our points across, sway people with what we feel is the right educational practice, and let people know who we are and what we stand for. We work to gain their trust and confidence because trust and confidence are the foundations of all relationships. That is the life of a leader. In a humble manner, with respect, courtesy, and dignity for all, you become the "influencer" that people come to know and depend upon for counsel and example.

Your leader influence may be in the classroom helping students on a daily basis or in a building administrative role helping teachers reach their potential. It may be in the central office ensuring that curriculums, policy, protocols and financing are in place. Wherever you are, the power of your influence reaches out to others. It may cause the school custodian to have a better day or even a better life. The power of your influence may last an instant and just put a smile on your secretary's face or it may put an indelible mark on a child that sets that student a new course for life. The power of your influence may cause a paradigm shift in an entire school or district. The power of your influence may also cost you your job one day and cause your life to be altered in a way that you had never anticipated. Whatever the power of your influence, just come to realize that it is there and can manifest itself at times when you least expect it. At the end of the day, the question to be asked is simple: How many people's lives have you altered for the better?

During the course of our work, self-doubt can raise its ugly head. It is a demon that we probably all face at different times during our lives. Trust that you are doing the best you can for your students and staff. Trust that you are a good role model. Trust that what you do every day counts and makes a difference. Trust that your hard work and efforts, whether they are a lifetime in one district or a short stint in many, count. Trust that while the rewards of your venture may not be financial that at the end of your "stay," you will have made a difference. And trust that when you move on, people will ask you to leave them your forwarding address.

Leave Your (Trade) Mark.

In between being a teacher and an administrator, I spent two years in the world of print advertising. For most of that time I worked for an educational publication, *Instructor Magazine*, in the late 1970s. One of the many things that I learned working for *Instructor Magazine* was the power of advertising—the real influence of advertising in getting one's message to other people—be it print, audio, or in an audiovisual format. Companies use logos, signs, emblems, icons, mascots, and slogans to help get their message out to create customer awareness, loyalty, and product satisfaction. Companies, as well as political and religious groups, nonprofit organizations, and others, spend huge sums of money, worldwide in the hundreds of billions annually, in the field of advertising for one reason—it has the potential to pay off. It can lure new customers to a product or reinforce product value with existing ones. Some symbols, like the ones used by the Red Cross, Coca-Cola, and McDonalds, even have worldwide notoriety. (As an aside, advertising was always one of my favorite units to teach. Students can really get into learning about and relating to this topic.)

In schools we tend to have mascots as symbols to help create school spirit. Sometimes as school leaders we wear items that help reinforce that school spirit. However, ponder this question. How can *you* distinguish yourself from everyone else?

Over the years the following people have distinguished themselves while becoming associated with certain tangible items:

- George Burns and Groucho Marx (for us older folk)—cigars
- Clara Barton—Red Cross pin
- Lone Ranger—silver bullet and black mask
- Jacqueline Kennedy—pillbox hat
- Abe Lincoln—stovepipe hat
- Audrey Hepburn—black hat and glasses
- The Beatles—bowl haircuts
- Elvis Presley—sideburns
- Lucille Ball—red hair
- Johnny Cash—the man in black (wore black)
- Imelda Marcos—shoes
- Madeline Hunter—"anticipatory set"
- Linus—blanket

As noted in an earlier tip, for more than two decades I wore a different lapel pin to school every day and I became known as the "pin man." The pin would have daily significance. It always represented something positive, for example, patriotism, children, academic subjects. I would try to match the pin with an event or thought of the day. For example, if my student council was meeting I would wear my student council pin. If there was a play I would wear a drama pin.

On a separate note with respect to another little quirk (although this may be very common), I would place a smiley face inside one of the letters of my name when writing my signature. When writing a message I would occasionally even place the smiley face inside the name of a student. For example, when sending middle school students their back-to-school class schedules, I would write personal notes to each of them and place the "face" in their name. Although some may think this is a bit primary, it became known as a positive trademark, along with the lapel pins, that set me apart from a crowded field of adults. The most important element to me was that these items were terms of endearment and, in the course of time, became known as symbols of student advocacy, student centeredness, and student caring. They were physical symbols representing a commitment to children first, as well as having a positive outlook on life. They were my child advocate advertising amenities, although I will admit that at the time I didn't think of them in that way. I just enjoyed pins and smiley faces.

People have their languages. Countries have their flags. But what do *you* have that sends a message that *you* are a child advocate and care deeply? Thoughts, words, and deeds are obviously the most important display of child advocacy. However, like your signature, create a signature trait or trademark from which to be remembered.

Look Like a Professional.

Do you have the look? You know, the daily appearance of a school leader look? It's the professional and acceptable attire and grooming expected in the world of school leadership. Although administrative apparel may seem obvious to some, in a profession dominated mostly by women, it is important to note that dress and grooming can be extremely important to those who wish to convey the proper school leader image regardless of gender.

Sometimes the evolution from teacher to teacher-leader or administrator means examining the wardrobe and saying goodbye to the flip-flops, miniskirts, t-shirts, cargo pants, and sport jerseys as you enter the school building in the morning. The norms of dress change when one changes level of responsibility and it seems like an unnecessary risk to challenge observers as an inappropriately dressed *fashionista*. In some cases, personal reflection is needed on your appearance, so make sure to match your clothing to the message you wish to convey for the day: business today means business attire; no business today means jeans and a shirt or blouse. Although multiple body piercing and tattoos may be popular with the younger generation, they probably will not be accepted in many schools, which transfers to the point that neither will you. The conservative and traditional nature of schools will expect that visible piercing be removed and tattoos be covered.

But what about Casual Fridays, Kick-Back Days, and Blue Jean Day once a month on those months that don't end in "er?" My advice is one of caution and careful wardrobe selection and making sure you have a change of clothes in case an emergency meeting is called or you have a parent group meeting in the evening. Even though you know it is a special carefree clothing day, others may perceive your image as sloppy and slipshod and make incorrect inferences and assumptions about you from your attire.

I can think of one occasion when I really misjudged "the look." As a principal, I was expected to attend all school board meetings and our school board met twice a month. One cold and snowy evening, I arrived at the board meeting in a dark fur coat. I chose to wear it because it was the warmest thing I owned and I knew the walk from the car to the building and back again would be cold and freezing. After the meeting, the superintendent came up to me and quietly said, "Don't ever wear that coat to another school board meeting again!" I had really missed the boat when it came to the image I was sending. I stood out in the crowd and projected an image of wealth. The hidden message that could have been perceived by the board and community members attending the meeting was, "WOW, look at that coat. We must pay our administrators way too much." You can bet I never wore that coat to any school function again.

Proper clothing for school leaders and managing your professional image through dress should not be underestimated. It is the nonverbal communication that is at work here. You don't want to be the fellow in the flashy sports car who wears baggy pants or the lady in stiletto heels with the hot pink handbag. Very few school leaders that I have known can get away with that image. On the other hand, you don't want the fashion police to be called because you are wearing an outfit that should have been given away. Most school leaders I know match their clothing to the message they are trying to send. People should remember your ideas not your clothes. Honor yourself by not letting your sports jacket or tight fitting clothes speak louder than the vision you have for your school. *You* look fabulous should mean your clothing is understated, unassuming, appropriate, and not distracting.

Make a Difference in the Lives of Your Students.

It never fails. I hear it during interview sessions and heard it most recently when talking to and teaching prospective school leaders. What I regularly hear is a common philosophy that draws people into the field of education—a chance to make a difference in the lives of students. When interviewing a candidate for a teaching position a frequent question might be, "Why did you become a teacher?" When talking to a prospective school leader who is looking to their next position the conversation might turn toward, "How has your philosophy of education changed or remained the same as you look to becoming a leader?" Both questions are usually answered in a similar fashion. "I wanted to become a teacher (school leader) because I want to make a difference in the lives of students." Rarely do you hear, "Because I want to make a lot of money." Making a difference in the lives of students does seem to be a common mantra for those who enter the field of education. But how can one person make a difference in the lives of so many students?

We are already being asked to make a difference by limiting our gasoline consumption to conserve fuel. We are asked to make a difference in pollution by recycling. We are asked to *Go Green* in the media. With all that we are asked to do to make a difference with things, it seems perfectly logical that in a people business, such as education, a school leader should work toward making a difference in the lives of students. But isn't that a tall order?

The difference you make begins with your leadership and the strength and confidence you gain every day in the position. Each day's experience moves you closer to taking important steps in making a difference in a child's life. Many important people can point to a teacher who made a difference in their lives by aiming them in the right direction, setting them on a life path, developing new aspirations or encouraging them to really work hard at something. A school leader needs to look for a chance to be that special person for someone. From my experience simply bringing a smile to the face of a child can make a difference in a life.

How do we know we have made a difference? Well, there are signs. One sign came to me just recently in a photograph given to me by a relative. It was a picture of Richie and me at his kindergarten graduation. Richie had his homemade paper graduation hat on and was holding his rolled up paper diploma. I had my arm around him and his face displayed his "say cheese smile." Richie who is twenty-eight years old now had saved the picture and given it to my relative with the comment that he still remembered how happy he felt that graduation day. As his principal, he wondered how I was doing. After all those years, being remembered was a sign that I had made a positive difference in his life. I certainly chuckled at seeing the picture and felt a sense of pride. Where did the time go?

How do we know we have made a difference? It is still a hard question to answer and school leaders continually need to ask themselves that question and reflect upon the answers. Approach every situation as unique, as are the individuals involved, and process the information carefully and accurately. Conduct yourself as a true professional and worthy of being called a role model. A school leader is a principled teacher guiding, mentoring, and leading the way. One person can make a difference. You can be that one person.

Plan a Vacation a Year in Advance.

My wife of thirty-six years and I grew up a few miles apart. We knew the city of Chicago well, but not much beyond that. As such, one thing we had in common was that neither of us as a child had ever gone on a family vacation. At the time it seemed very normal. Fathers worked two jobs or double shifts just to make ends meet. I am reminded of the 1960s song *Five O'Clock World* by the Vogues. It opens like this:

> Up every mornin' just to keep my job
> I gotta fight my way through the hustling mob
> Sounds of the city poundin' in my brain
> While another days goes down the drain (yeah, yeah).

While neither of our fathers came home at five, closer to ten was the norm, the daily grind of a job, no matter how many hours one spends there, can be wearing—even if one enjoys it. As I got older I felt badly that our parents never enjoyed a vacation, not only because of the fun associated with a vacation and the fond memories that can come from a vacation, but also the health benefits related to taking a vacation. One picture, just one picture is all you need, of an enjoyable, relaxing vacation can be therapeutic. That picture can say a thousand words.

The challenge we face in schools is that we could work sixteen hours a day, seven days a week and never be done. The job of a school leader, whether it is program improvement, differentiating lessons, preparing school board reports, or just responding to the daily grind, can consume you. We need a break; we deserve a break.

There are several things to think about when considering a vacation. Here are some of them.

- *Define your vacation*—A vacation shouldn't just mean time away from work. Granted it is a rest period but we all differ on what we consider a "rest period" or time away. My wife always considered a rest period just that—time to sit and relax, preferably by a pool, and read a book. I would consider a rest period running around and viewing exhibits. I was the most unpopular father when one year our "vacation" was visiting several local museums and taking notes. Think about what you want from a vacation, define it, and be able to describe what it means to you. A vacation can be staying at home and relaxing. It could be zip lining or lying around a swimming pool.
- *Plan your vacation a year in advance*—Besides the opportunity to save for a vacation and the economic advantages usually associated with early decision making, I see the main advantage of early planning as being the mental daily anticipation of knowing one is going on a vacation. One really has something to look forward to and can plan for, research and think about regularly. It's a vacation that keeps on giving. It's the thought that counts.

- *Think about when is the right time to take a vacation*—Some of us just need that break during the school year, whereas others may use the summer to get away. If you go during the summer there is one advantage. You can answer the proverbial back-to-school question, which bugged the heck out of me: So what did you do all summer?
- *Decide what you can afford*—A vacation does not have to mean going to Europe or Hawaii. For years when our children were young, my wife and I would take our children to Wisconsin for just a few days. It wasn't expensive and it was very memorable. Staying home can be just fine, too. It all depends on what you do and how you define a vacation.
- *Decide how long your vacation should be*—Although this has monetary implications, the length of a vacation is really critical. While any time off is better than no time off, some of us need several days to really get "mentally" away. The amount of vacation time allotted varies not only from place of employment to place of employment, but even from country to country.
- *Take the vacation with friends*—Going with friends can be a special added bonus to the trip. Unless you are looking to go alone or with your spouse or significant other, being on a vacation with close friends can provide increased opportunities for early planning discussions, vacationing conversations, and overall enjoyment. Just make sure you choose friends with whom you are "vacation compatible." My wife and I have gone on several short vacations (three to four days) with our friends, Lyn and Frank. The vacations have become vacations that kept on giving as we have laughed and talked about them years later.
- *Decide how much vacation-communication you want*—It has been said when traveling, take more money and fewer clothes. But no matter whether you are staying at home or going away, plan in advance how much you want to be in touch with work. Having laptops and cell phones make it easy to be in constant communication but is that what you really want? It might be better to make communication one-way, from you first, unless a critical matter arises. I personally had a very difficult time changing my voice mail message to "I will be out of the office until…," but learned to do so. I also learned that people want you to take a vacation. (In my case it probably was just to get rid of me for a while!)

Take a vacation. You deserve it and you will come back with your mental and physical batteries fully charged and ready for what comes your way. So plan that vacation early and reap the benefits all year long.

Safeguard the Public Trust by Remembering You Are *In Loco Parentis.*

In loco parentis is a Latin phrase that means, "in place of the parent." The doctrine *in loco parentis* has a rich and interesting history that dates back to eighteenth century English common law. During that time, when teachers felt the need to administer corporal punishment, they were protected by law because they were acting on behalf of a child's parent. This doctrine should not be a new concept to school leaders. School administration preparation programs introduce students to this concept in several courses. Legal guardians have *in loco parentis* status when taking on the commitment of raising children who are not biologically their own. However, the most common application relates to teachers, students, and school administrators. Schools can act in ways that are reserved only for parents and families.

But *in loco parentis* brings with it different complications when applying it to today's school context. There are some parents who don't want *you* to be the parent for their child because they will take care of anything the child needs from tutors to discipline. With some parents, I used to worry about the child after making a call home about a discipline issue. I would fear that the child would be physically punished after my call, so I would carefully construct my words and tell the parent that I was just informing them of the incident and I would be happy to take care of the matter at school when it was appropriate to do so. The parent was usually pleased and relieved that they did not have to do anything at home. Even today there are some parents who give you permission to use physical force on their children if needed—sad but true.

Then there are parents who want *you* to be the parent. They may ask you, "What should I do?" or "What would you do if you were me?" or "I can't do anything with this child, maybe you can." or "I am done being Mary's parent." On some occasions, they are unavailable or too busy to parent. Whatever the excuse, they look to you to be the parent.

Acting in place of a parent in today's schools can be messy and complicated especially in the areas of discipline, dress, searching lockers and school bags, and dealing with personal property, such as cell phones and purses, just to mention a few items. Before and after school programs for children who might ordinarily go home to an empty house extends the purpose of schooling to accommodate working parents, but can also be problematic and thorny for school leaders. Then there are chronically tardy and truant students whose parents look to the school for advice and resolutions. Some critics question how far the school can go with *in loco parentis*. I see it not as a question of how far, but has the school gone far enough in its supportive role for youngsters.

Guard, protect, and care for youngsters, as any responsible parent would want you to. Carry this mindset with you into your decision making and problem solving. When making a decision between two competing factors, place the impact on the life of the child first. One example that begs for child advocacy is placing students in various leveled classes like basic, honors, gifted, and advanced placement. So often a test score or recommendation is the only consideration variable. Put on your parent–school leader hat and follow through in your thinking about other factors that should be considered in the placement.

So what does *in loco parentis* really mean? Are you ready to go loco? Honor yourself with this significant role that has been bestowed upon you and value it as the most important and delicate aspects of your work. It is a constant caring and advocacy role. After all, you might be the only advocate a child has.

References

APA survey finds rising stress takes toll. (2007). Retrieved January 19, 2009 from http://www.apapractice.org/apo/in_the_news/apa_survey_finds_rising.html.

Barth, R. (1990). *Improving schools from within.* San Francisco, CA: Jossey-Bass.

Bolman, L. G., and Deal, T. E. (2003). *Reframing organizations: Artistry, choice, leadership.* San Francisco, CA: Jossey-Bass.

Bolman, L. G., and Deal, T.E. (2002, February). Leading with soul and spirit. *School Administrator, 59*(2), 21–26.

Brayman, C., and Fink, D. (2006, February). School leadership succession and the challenges of change. *Educational Administration Quarterly, 42*(1), 62–89.

Burns, J.M. (1997). *Leadership.* New York: Harper & Row.

Byrd, J., Drews, C., and Johnson, J. (2006, August). Factors impacting superintendent turnover: Lessons from the field. *NCPEA Education Review, 7*(2), 1–13.

C4's UChoose40: One Hit Wonders. (2009). Retrieved from http://en.wikipedia.org/wiki/One-hit_wonder.

Deming, W.E. (1997). Quality leaders. In K. Shelton (Ed.), *A new paradigm of leadership* (pp.121–126). Provo, UT: Executive Excellence.

Doud, J. L., and Keller, E. P. (1998, September). The K-8 principal in 1998. *Principal, 78*(1), 5–6.

Edelman, M.J. (1977). *The symbolic uses of politics.* Madison: The University of Wisconsin Press.

Fullan, M. (2003). *The moral imperative of school leadership.* Thousand Oaks, CA: Corwin Press.

Gardner, H. (1995). *Leading minds.* New York: Basic Books.

Glass, T.E., and Franceschini, L. (2007). *The state of the American school superintendent: A mid-decade study.* Lanham, MD: Rowan & Littlefield.

Goleman, D. (1998, November-December). What makes a good leader? *Harvard Business Review, 76*(6), 93–104.

Goleman, D. (1995). *Emotional intelligence.* New York: Bantam Books.

Gootman, E. (2006, May 22). Heavy turnover in New York's principal ranks. *The New York Times.* Retrieved October 20, 2008 from http://www.nytimes.com/2006/05/22nyregion/22nyregion/22principals.html.

Hargreaves, A., and Fullan, M. (1988). *What's worth fighting for out there?* New York: Teachers College Press.

Harvey, T., and Donaldson, G. (2003, September-October). Professional vitality. *Principal, 83*(1), 30–33.

Hertling, E. (2001, April). Retaining principals. Clearinghouse on Educational Policy and Management (CEPM). *Eric Digest #147.* Retrieved October 9, 2008 from http://uoregon.edu/publications/digests/digest 147.html.

Kelehear, Z. (2004, November). Controlling stress. *Principal Leadership, 5*(3), 30–3.

Kimbrough, R. B., and Nunnery, M. Y. (1988). *Educational administration,* 3rd ed. New York: Macmillan.

Kopkowski, C. (2008, February). *Why they leave: Lack of respect, NCLB, and underfunding—In a topsy-turvy profession, what can make today's teachers stay?* NEA Today Teacher Retention. Retrieved January 27, 2009 from http://www.nea.org:80/home/12630.htm.

Kowalski, T. J. (2004). *Public relations in schools.* Upper Saddle River, NJ: Pearson.

Lambert, L. (1998). *Building leadership capacity in schools.* Alexandria, VA: ASCD.

Lortie, D. (2009). *School principal: Managing in public.* Chicago: University of Chicago Press.

Merriam-Webster's Collegiate Dictionary, 11th ed. (2003). Springfield, MA: Merriam-Webster.

McCormack, M. H. (2000). *Getting results for dummies.* Foster City, CA: IDG Books.

Mihans, R. (2008, June). Can teachers lead teachers? *Phi Delta Kappan, 90*(1), 762–765.

NAESP Leadership Academy, October 27, 2009. personal communication.

Paine, T. (1918) *Common sense.* New York: Peter Eckler.

Peterson, K. (2002, Summer). Positive or negative. *Journal of Staff Development, 23*(3), 10–15.

President's Commission on Mental Health, (1978). *Report of the President's Commission on Mental Health.* Washington, DC: United States Government Printing Office.

Rosborg, J., McGee, M. and Burgett, J. (2003). *What every superintendent and principal needs to know: School leadership for the real world.* Santa Maria, CA: Education Communication Unlimited.

Sapolsky, R. (2004). *Why zebras don't get ulcers.* New York: Holt.

Schoolyard ecology leader's handbook. (2009). Retrieved April 16, 2009 from http://www.ecostudies.org/syefest/ap1res13.htm.

Sergiovanni, T. J. (2005). *Strengthening the heartbeat: Leading and learning together in schools.* San Francisco: Jossey-Bass.

Schon, D. (1984). *The reflective practitioner: How professionals think in action.* New York: Basic Books.

Taylor, B. (2008). *Urban school superintendents are hard to keep.* Retrieved October 14, 2008 from http://www.usatoday.com/news/education.

Teacher retention, attrition, and mobility studies. (2006). Retrieved January 28, 2009. from http://www.retainingteachers.com.

Troher, K. (2007, March 24). *Wilmont-Trevor staff come to the rescue during administrator's cardiac arrest* (p 1). Kenosha, WI: Kenosha News.

University Council for Educational Administration. (2008, March). *Implications from UCEA: The revolving door of the principalship.* Retrieved October 9, 2008 from http://www.ecea.org.

USA TODAY. (2008). *Urban school superintendents are hard to keep.* Retrieved October 14, 2008 from http://www.usatoday.com/news/education.

Win control over stress in your life. Tools for happier lives. Retrieved January 19, 2009 from http://www.amyoclinic.com/health/stress/SR00001.

For Product Safety Concerns and Information please contact our EU
representative GPSR@taylorandfrancis.com
Taylor & Francis Verlag GmbH, Kaufingerstraße 24, 80331 München, Germany

www.ingramcontent.com/pod-product-compliance
Lightning Source LLC
Chambersburg PA
CBHW080938300426
44115CB00017B/2867